THE KNOWLEDGE ECONOMY

THE KNOWLEDGE ECONOMY

Roberto Mangabeira Unger

VERSO
London • New York

First published in English by Verso 2019
© Roberto Mangabeira Unger 2019

1 3 5 7 9 10 8 6 4 2

Verso
UK: 6 Meard Street, London W1F 0EG
US: 20 Jay Street, Suite 1010, Brooklyn, NY 11201

versobooks.com

Verso is the imprint of New Left Books

ISBN-13: 978-1-78873-497-4
ISBN-13: 978-1-78873-500-1 (US EBK)
ISBN-13: 978-1-78873-499-8 (UK EBK)

British Library Cataloguing in Publication Data
A catalogue record for this book is available from the British Library

Library of Congress Cataloging-in-Publication Data
A catalog record for this book is available from the Library of Congress

Typeset in Minion Pro by Hewer Text UK Ltd, Edinburgh
Printed and bound by CPI Group (UK) Ltd, Croydon, CR0 4YY

Contents

1.

The Most Advanced
Practice of Production

A new practice of production has emerged in all the major economies of the world. The simplest and most telling of its many names is the knowledge economy. We might also call it the experimental economy to highlight its most characteristic attitude toward its own work. The knowledge economy holds the promise of changing, to our benefit, some of the most deep-seated and universal features of economic life and of dramatically enhancing productivity and growth.

Its effects have, however, so far proved modest. Instead of spreading widely, it has remained restricted to vanguards of production, employing few workers. Entrepreneurial and technological elites control it. A handful of large global firms have reaped the lion's share of the profits that it has so far yielded. It appears in every part of the production system; the habit of equating it with high-technology industry is unwarranted. In every sector of the economy, however, it remains a narrow fringe, excluding the vast majority of the labor force. Even though its products are used ever more widely, its revolutionary practices continue to be quarantined.

If only we could find a path from these insular vanguards to socially inclusive ones we would have built a powerful motor of economic growth. We would also have supplied an antidote to inequality far more forceful than the after-the-fact correction, by progressive taxation and redistributive social spending, of inequalities generated within established market regimes. The true character and potential of the new practice of production remain disguised: by virtue of being insular, the knowledge economy is also undeveloped. The technologies with which it has been most recently associated, such as robots and artificial intelligence, have riveted worldwide attention. Nevertheless, we have barely begun to grasp its significance for economic and social life or gained insight into its possible futures.

This book presents a view of the knowledge economy, of the causes and consequences of its confinement, and of the passage from its present insularity to its possible inclusiveness. The established body of economic ideas is useful, and even indispensable, but it is also insufficient for an understanding of these problems. Received economic theory leaves us short of the insights that we need to guide the institutional and policy changes required to take us from the insular knowledge economy that we have to the inclusive one that we need. The effort to think through the agenda of an inclusive vanguardism prompts us to reassess the alternative futures of economics as well as the alternative futures of the economy.

This situation in economic reality and in economic thought confronts all nations, especially developing countries, with a dilemma that has now come to the forefront of practical political economy. Conventional industrialization, as a guarantee of economic growth and of convergence to the level of the richest economies, has stopped working. However, the alternative—the advancement of a broad-based, economy-wide form of the knowledge economy—seems to be inaccessible. Not even the richest economies, with the most educated populations, have achieved it. Is it not a goal beyond reach for the rest of the world?

In every moment of economic history, there is a most advanced practice of production. It may not be, when it first appears and begins to spread, the most efficient practice: the one that achieves the greatest output relative to the inputs required. It is, however, the most promising practice: the one with the greatest potential to reach and to stay at the frontier of productivity, and to inspire change across the economy. It possesses, in higher measure than rival practices of production, the attributes of fecundity and versatility, attributes that assume varied forms in different settings.

In the past, the most advanced practice of production has been associated with a particular sector of the economy: manufacturing, for example, in contrast to agriculture or services. However, the most advanced practice may appear, instead, as a piece of many sectors rather than remaining identified with only one.

The two greatest thinkers in the history of economics—Adam Smith and Karl Marx—believed that the best way to discover the deepest truths of economics was to study the most advanced practice of production. For them, it was mechanized manufacturing as it had appeared in the early years of the Industrial Revolution of the late eighteenth century, to be followed by the industrial mass production of the later nineteenth century. Smith and Marx were right to take the study of the most advanced practice as the gateway to economic insight.

The study of the most advanced practice of production is the most rewarding source of insight into the workings of the economy and its possible futures because the most advanced practice is the variant of economic activity that most fully reveals our powers. Just as the most advanced practice changes over time, as one most advanced practice succeeds another, so does our conception of what makes a practice more advanced than its predecessors also shift. In the light of the most advanced practice of our time, we change ideas about how economies do and can work. We reconsider the whole of economic history.

To today's most advanced practice of production I give the familiar label the knowledge economy and go on to characterize it, explain it, and explore its alternative futures. Our encounter with the knowledge economy suggests a new criterion for what makes a practice of production the most advanced. In one sense, it is the practice of production that is closest to the mind, and especially to the part of our mental life that we call the imagination. In another sense, this most mindful practice is the one that, among all available forms of economic activity, most intimately and continuously connects our experiments in using and transforming nature and our experiments in cooperating. It connects them by using each of these sets of experiments to stimulate the other. One of the best ways to think about technology is to view it as an expression of the marriage between these two kinds of experiments: the ones that change nature and the ones that change how we work together.

As we look back on economic history from the vantage point of the knowledge economy, we can see earlier most advanced practices of production with new eyes. Each of them was also the most mindful practice of its time and the one that brought most closely together our experiments in mobilizing nature for our benefit and our experiments in changing the way in which we cooperate in production. These reasons for the distinction enjoyed by the most advanced practice of production show why it is the practice that best reveals our characteristic powers: those that make us who we are. No wonder that studying it is the quickest and most reliable route to the development of economic theory.

We are accustomed to seeing the history of our economic activity as a field of pitiless constraint, in which scarcity, need, dependence, and coercion play major roles. From the perspective of the emergence of the knowledge economy, however, economic life has also always been a story of the troubled advance of the imagination.

The central idea of this book is that the now most advanced practice of production has the potential to radically alter human life. It can mark a momentous change in the character of economic activity.

We fail to recognize this potential, or see it only in its most superficial expression: the impact of the new technologies associated with information, communication, and the internet. What explains our failure to understand the nature and reach of the new most advanced practice of production is that we know it only in a confined form. It has not spread widely in the economy; it remains restricted to insular vanguards of production in the control of an entrepreneurial and technological elite. And it therefore fails to reveal its full potential.

The depth of an advanced practice of production—the degree to which it develops and realizes its potential—is related to its scope: the extent to which it is disseminated throughout the economy. It is only by appearing in many contexts and adapting to the distinct opportunities and constraints presented by each of them that a practice of production develops, allowing us to discern its deeper, more far-reaching attributes under the surface of its shallower expressions.

The knowledge economy is confined, but it is no longer restricted to any particular sector of production. It does not even have a privileged association with industry, in contrast to services or agriculture, as mechanized manufacturing and industrial mass production did. It exists in every sector—in knowledge-intensive services and precision, scientific agriculture as well as in high-technology industry. Nevertheless, in each sector it appears as a fringe from which the vast majority of the labor force remains excluded.

Its operation is controlled by a small number of large firms with increasingly worldwide presence. These firms have learned to routinize or commoditize much of their productive activity and then to contract these pieces out to businesses and factories in other parts of their world. The result is that the knowledge economy proper, the mind-rich way of producing with all the potentially revolutionary traits that I later explore, becomes an ever more restricted inner circle: a kingdom within a kingdom.

The inner kingdom and the routinized periphery of the present global but insular form of the knowledge economy sell widely their products and services as well as access to their platforms and networks. Firms and individuals in every corner of society use them. However, it is not by using these products and services that a firm or an individual comes to share in the most advanced practice of production. A firm may use the product or service to do its work more efficiently—for example, by deploying computer networks and their related software to manage complex information—without sharing in what I shall describe as the defining features of the now most advanced practice of production. The firm may even employ efficiency-enhancing gadgets as a way to forestall rather than to initiate the changes that would turn it into a protagonist of the knowledge economy.

The central thesis of this book is that many of our most important material and moral interests depend on whether the knowledge economy—the now most advanced practice of production—will continue to be confined to insular vanguards, advanced fringes within each sector of the economy. The knowledge economy can turn into an inclusive rather than an insular vanguard. Its dissemination, however, requires change in our basic economic arrangements and assumptions: not simply a different way of regulating the market economy or of doing business under its present institutions—but a different kind of market economy. There must then begin a dispute to which we are unaccustomed: not about the relative proportions of market and state but about the institutional arrangements by which we organize decentralized economic activity.

I call the knowledge economy restricted to the advanced fringes in which it now prospers insular or confined vanguardism, and the knowledge economy widely disseminated inclusive vanguardism. The choice between insular and inclusive vanguardism is fateful. It touches on all of our economic and on many of our political and even spiritual concerns. It bears on our chances of more fully realizing in practice the ideal that commands the greatest authority in the world and the strongest kinship to democracy: the ideal of effective agency, of the ability of every man and woman to act upon the circumstances of his or her existence.

The goal of establishing an inclusive vanguardism—an economy-wide version of the most advanced practice of production—bears directly on the two overriding concerns of practical political economy: stagnation and inequality. A widespread and developed form of the knowledge economy offers the most promising way to promote socially inclusive economic growth and to diminish economic inequality.

Under Alvin Hansen's old label of "secular stagnation," many economists have proposed to explain in recent years the persistent slowdown of economic growth. The figures measuring the growth of productivity chart the dimension of this slowdown. Consider the well-studied example of the US economy. From 1947 to 1972, labor productivity, which roughly tracks total factor productivity, rose in the United States by an average of 2.8 percent a year; from 1972 to 1994 by 1.5 percent a year; from 1994 to 2005 by 2.8 percent a year; and from 2005 to the present by 1.4 percent a year. After a period of slow growth, productivity spiked in 1994–2005 and then fell back again.

The slowdown in the growth of productivity since 1972, interrupted only by the turn-of-the-century spike, has been attributed to many of the factors emphasized by Hansen in the 1930s: the decline of population growth, the inadequacy of aggregate demand, and a "savings glut"—an excess of savings over consumption. One factor, however, largely absent from the older discussion of secular stagnation, has now taken center stage: the supposedly more limited transformative effect of contemporary technologies, especially in communication and information, when compared to the technological innovations of a hundred years ago. Consistently with this line of argument, we can explain the temporary rise in productivity growth in 1994–2005 as the result of a one-time phenomenon: the adoption of computers and other digital technologies by a wide range of mega-, large-, and medium-sized firms whose operations otherwise bear few traces of the now most advanced practice of production.

The effect of the secular stagnation thesis has been to cast on the decline of economic growth in general and of productivity growth in particular an undeserved halo of naturalness and necessity. There is no reason to believe that contemporary technologies are any less revolutionary in their potential than the mechanical innovations of a century ago; there is in fact better reason to suppose that we have barely begun to tap their potential and by tapping it to encourage the innovations that they may inspire. However, the effects of technologies are always mediated by the institutional and cultural settings in which they take place.

I conjecture that a major cause of economic stagnation in the period since the early 1970s has been the confinement of the knowledge economy to relatively insular vanguards rather than its economy-wide dissemination. There is nothing natural about this phenomenon: it presents a riddle requiring explanation.

Earlier most advanced practices of production—mechanized manufacturing and industrial mass production—set their mark on every part of economic life despite their close connection with one sector: industry. The knowledge economy should in principle be susceptible to even more widespread dissemination. Nothing about its characteristics limits it to any particular sector of the economy, which is why it has appeared in every sector, albeit only as fringe in each one.

Yet the opposite has happened: despite its appearance in many sectors it has remained in even the richest economies and the most educated societies an archipelago of islands alien to the main tenor of economic life around it. The consequence has been to deprive the economy and the labor force of the most powerful stimulus to the enhancement of productivity: one that would result not from machines alone but from a radicalization of our ability both to innovate and to cooperate—the promise of inclusive vanguardism. Success in developing and using contemporary technologies would be only one of many aspects of such an advance.

What the thesis of secular stagnation seeks to naturalize is, on this account, largely a consequence of our failure to free the advanced practice of production from its containment within the narrow segments of economic activity and the limited range of firms in which it now flourishes. We fail to recognize the extent of our loss because we have come, unjustifiably, to think of this insularity as natural and to mistake the deeper features of the most advanced practice of production for the characteristics of the part of the economy in which its presence has been most salient: high-technology industry.

The confinement of the knowledge economy to fringes in all sectors of production has similarly powerful implications for inequality. The distinction between an insular albeit multisectoral vanguard and the rest of the economy—a collection of rearguards—has become a powerful engine of inequality of opportunity and capability as well as of income and wealth.

In every economy, even the most developed with the most educated labor force, retrograde small business in services and retail (together with backward rural smallholdings wherever a significant proportion of the economically active population remains in agriculture) represents the largest part of this economic periphery. Such business remains the residual ideal and refuge of hundreds of millions of people. It is not only a last-ditch source of employment; it is also often the only accessible way to satisfy the nearly universal desire to achieve a modicum of prosperity and independence. Almost everywhere, small business, especially family small business, survives on the basis of family saving and self-exploitation. Almost always, with the exception of knowledge-intensive elite professional services and the partial exception of the traditional technical trades, it remains largely untouched by the characteristics of the advanced practice of production.

If small business is the primary component of the economic rearguard, the secondary component is declining mass-production industry. This industry and the services with which it has been historically associated are the seat of what used to be the most advanced practice. They arouse a degree of attention disproportionate to their significance by contrast to the inattention from which small business traditionally suffers.

Declining mass-production industry commands attention for several reasons. One reason is that the classic formula of development (expounded by the development economics of the second half of the twentieth century) has been to transfer workers from less productive to more productive sectors, with "more productive" understood to mean industry and "less productive" to mean agriculture. Another reason is that the representatives of the industrial labor force in the labor movement and in politics have played a leading role in left-leaning political parties around the world. Yet another reason is that right wing parties have recognized in the dispossession and insecurity of workers in mass-production industry a chance to broaden and reshape their social base.

A common impulse throughout the world has been to abandon small business to its own devices, notwithstanding a panoply of minor concessions to its interests, while accepting the regressive and relatively unproductive character of its practices as natural or even inevitable. Another common impulse has been to protect national mass-production industry against foreign competition, including wage competition, with no hint of any plan to convert it to the practices, and conform it to the requirements, of the knowledge economy.

As new wealth accumulates in the knowledge economy, the distance separating this economy from the vast periphery of production generates inequalities that the traditional devices for attenuating inequality are inadequate to master. These devices are the protection of traditional small business and compensatory redistribution by tax and transfer: progressive taxation and redistributive social spending. They give rise to a secondary distribution of economic advantage by contrast to the arrangements shaping the primary distribution.

Such after-the-fact correction is likely to have only a marginal effect on inequality rooted in the organization of the economy and especially in the structure of production. These corrective initiatives change only the demand side of the economy, leaving the supply side and the arrangements of production untouched. As a result, they can never become large and consequential enough without disturbing established incentives to save, invest, and employ. The familiar opposition of arguments from efficiency and from equity is simply the rhetorical reflection of this imbalance between the task of moderating inequality and the methods chosen for doing so.

The development of an inclusive vanguardism—dealing with inequality of advantage on the supply as well as on the demand side of the economy—would represent the most effective antidote to the extremes of inequality as well as the most promising response to the slowing of growth in productivity. The exigent character of the requirements of such a form of the knowledge economy—in the dissemination of a new style of education, in the renewal of the moral culture of production, and in the reshaping of economic institutions— would ensure its profound effect on inequality. It would do so not by retrospective redistribution—the defining method of institutionally conservative social democracy—but by revising the arrangements that shape the primary distribution of economic advantage and produce inequality in the first place. It would attack inequality through the same devices by which it strikes stagnation.

In this book, I develop an argument about inclusive vanguardism in nine steps. In the first step, I characterize the knowledge economy, the now most advanced practice of production. In the second step, I discuss the enigma of its confinement to insular vanguards, the chief causes of this confinement, and its far-reaching effects on stagnation and inequality. In the third step, I address the requirements for the economy-wide dissemination of the most advanced practice of production. These requirements fall into three categories: the cognitive-educational, the social-moral, and the legal-institutional—a change in the institutional framework of the market order. In the fourth step, I speak to the nature of the culture and of the politics that forms the setting most hospitable to the fulfillment of those three sets of requirements.

Taken together, the third and the fourth steps of my argument present the project of an inclusive vanguardism, understood as a trajectory of cumulative change rather than as a blueprint or a system. In each instance, I suggest some of the initiatives and reforms by which, in the circumstances of contemporary economies, we can begin to move in this direction. The program of an inclusive vanguardism is both possible and necessary. The means by which to begin to develop it are already at hand. Its advancement represents the best response to both economic stagnation and economic inequality.

In the fifth step, I review the argument about confined and inclusive vanguardism from the perspective of the concerns of classical development economics, the chief recommendation of which was to boost economic growth by transferring workers and resources from relatively less productive agriculture to relatively more productive manufacturing, in the form that represented until recently the most advanced productive practice—industrial mass production. This formula is now broken, for many reasons that I shall examine, including competition from the global and versatile megafirms of the knowledge economy as well as from low-wage mass production (belated Fordism) in developing countries. But if the old formula of industrial mass production no longer works, the alternative of inclusive vanguardism seems to be beyond reach. If none of the richest economies have implemented or even conceived it, how can we expect it to be established in societies in which even the less demanding educational and institutional requirements of conventional mass production often remain unmet?

In the sixth step, I apply the view of the knowledge economy and its futures presented in this book to the political economy of the rich countries. Failure to develop a strategy of economic growth that makes the most productive practice widely available to the economically active population lies at the heart of many of the political-economic problems of the richest societies: faltering economic growth, the inadequacy of attempts to attenuate inequality that leave the hierarchical segmentation of the economy untouched, and the rise of politicians and political movements that give voice to an experience of dispossession but offer no prospect of structural change.

The program of an inclusive form of the knowledge economy can advance only as part of a movement changing education, culture, and politics, as well as innovating in the institutions of the market order. It therefore requires a break—even if achieved by gradual and fragmentary means—with the institutional and ideological settlement that has prevailed in these societies since the mid-twentieth century.

In the seventh step, I reconsider my account of confined and inclusive vanguardism from the perspective of the most rudimentary and familiar problem of economic theory: the relation between supply and demand. Economic growth remains subject to repeated interruptions, failures, and slumps because breakthroughs of constraints on supply do not automatically ensure corresponding breakthroughs of constraints on demand or vice versa. There is no way to implement through contract, at the level of the economy rather than of the firm, the bargain that Henry Ford half facetiously offered his workers: to pay them so well that they could buy his cars.

The solution to the accommodation of supply and demand at full employment is not contractual but institutional. Under the conditions of contemporary economies only an inclusive vanguardism—the most radical and encompassing form of breakthrough of the constraints on both supply and demand—can ensure that the growth of supply will be enough to sustain the growth of demand and the growth of demand to support the growth of supply. Keynes's doctrine deals with only a special case of such failures of accommodation between supply and demand, or of equilibrium, at a depressed level of employment.

In the eighth step of my argument, I discuss the character of the economic ideas that we need if we are to think through the agenda of inclusive vanguardism. I do so by exploring the uses and limitations of the main line of economic theory: the economics inaugurated by the marginalist theoreticians at the end of the nineteenth century. An alternative future of the knowledge economy—one that goes beyond the insular vanguardism of today—has as its counterpart an economics with more resources than the powerful analytical tools forged by the marginalists. Its explanatory and transformative ambitions must differ from theirs.

In the ninth and last step, I address the higher purpose of a knowledge economy that becomes inclusive and progresses toward the limit of its potential: the promise of a better chance to live larger lives and to become bigger together.

This book is a sketch both as a program and as an exercise in economic analysis. It is an attempt to imagine an alternative direction for the knowledge economy and to exemplify a way of thinking on which such a direction can draw.

The theme of confined and inclusive vanguardism—or of the alternative futures of the knowledge economy— leads by many routes to the central issues of political economy today. It requires us to think in ways for which there is no readily available method or model. The reward as a program is the prospect of an advance in our ability to give practical consequence to the most widely professed political-economic goal in the world today: the goal of socially inclusive economic growth. The reward as a way of thinking is the promise that, like Smith and Marx, we might use the study of the most advanced practice of production to achieve deeper insight into the economy and its transformation.

2.

The Knowledge Economy: Its Characteristics Described at the Level of Management and Production Engineering

We know the knowledge economy now under constraint in the form of the islands and fringes that it occupies in each sector of the economy. We are tempted to identify it with its most familiar form: high-technology industry, especially as pursued by a handful of global mega firms and by a periphery of start-up businesses.

Alternatively, we confuse it with the use of its products and services, as when firms of any scale take advantage of these products and services—notably computers and other information technologies—to organize complex information and enhance the efficiency of their work without otherwise changing how they operate. The telltale sign that such use captures only a small portion of the potential of the new practice of production is that it is likely to provide a one-time boost to productivity, the effect of which is soon exhausted. Such was the change that helps account for the temporary boost in productivity in the United States from 1994 to 2005: a wave of adoption of digital technology to improve efficiency by managing information supplied the one-time boost.

To grasp the true character of the most advanced practice of production, we must imagine it widely disseminated and deepened or radicalized through such dissemination. It shows its character and potential by developing across a wide range of economic activities.

By a first approximation the knowledge economy is the accumulation of capital, technology, technology-relevant capabilities, and science in the conduct of productive activity. Its characteristic ideal is permanent innovation in procedures and methods as well as in products and technologies. It does not want to be just another way of producing goods and services, with distinctive technological equipment. It wants to be a paradigm of production that keeps reinventing itself. What this ideal means we can now see first at the narrow level of management, coordination, and production, and then in three deeper attributes. These traits describe the knowledge economy not as it exists now but as it would exist once disseminated and radicalized.

Viewed from the limited and relatively superficial perspective of management and production engineering, the knowledge economy is the practice that reconciles production at large scale with "destandardization" or customization and the maintenance of coherence and momentum in the planning of production with decentralization of initiative. These achievements can mean little or much, depending on how far they are taken. They can represent marginal enhancements of efficiency and stratagems to motivate workers by affording them greater room for both individual initiative and teamwork without reshaping property and power in the firm. Or they can form part of a cumulative and consequential change in the organization of work and ultimately in the regime of property. Thus, both the expression and the development of these more superficial features of the productive practice depend on the progress of the deeper characteristics that I later discuss.

Additive manufacturing (3D printers), robotics, and, more generally, flexible, numerically controlled machine tools make it possible to diversify products, exploring their possible variants, while combining such prodigal diversification with scale of production. The technological facility would amount to little if it failed to mobilize and develop a range of capabilities that shorten the distance between productive activity and experimental science. A 3D printer, for example, allows its user to move rapidly and continuously between the conception and the materialization of a product, and to revise the conception in light of discoveries made in the course of the materialization. Artificial intelligence goes further, making explicit what machines can do for us: everything that we have learned how to repeat so that with their help we can push ahead into the zone of the not yet repeatable.

Just as important as reconciling scale of production with exploratory product differentiation and variation is changing the way people work together: the technical division of labor. The point is to decentralize initiative without losing coherence and momentum. In any way of organizing work, there may seem to be an intractable tension, if not an outright contradiction, between the advantages of decentralized and discretionary initiative by individuals or groups and the maintenance of such momentum and coherence. The practices of the knowledge economy, even in its present insular form, attenuate this tension even when they fail to dissolve it.

One element of this practice is the assignment of tasks to work teams enjoying wide latitude in how they organize their work (e.g., the "Toyota method of production"). Another element is an approach to coordinating the activities of these teams that tempers central managerial direction with the collaborative development and revision of the production plan by the teams and their leaders. The result is a superior, more flexible form of order, better able to identify opportunities for improvement and to learn from experience.

Technology alone is insufficient to ensure the marriage of scale with differentiation and of coordinated forward movement with decentralized initiative. Its use must be enveloped in practices and attitudes that point in the direction of deeper changes in the way of working and ultimately in the institutional arrangements of the economy as well as in the education and culture of the participants in the work of production.

The combination of scale with almost limitless product differentiation or customization presupposes a way of understanding and developing a business that seeks to create new demands, classes of consumers, and markets rather than taking the demand for its products as an exogenous and inalterable datum. The desire for the differentiation of goods and services may be elastic, as the consumer is surprised by new options, as the industrial production for a mass market takes on some of the features of craft production for an elite, and as the distinction between manufacturing and services breaks down. Advanced manufacturing may not only sell its products bundled with services; it consists to a large extent of crystallized intellectual services.

The reconciliation of decentralized initiative with persistence in a coordinated production plan is incompatible with a command-and-control approach to the organization of work. It requires a change in the character of the technical division of labor: the way in which participants in the production process cooperate. There must be no stark contrast between supervisory and implementing jobs: the plan of production must be continuously revised in the process of being implemented. The attenuation of the contrast between supervisory and implementing roles will have as its counterpart the relativization of all specialized implementing jobs. Such rigid specialization presupposes the stark contrast between conception and execution. The team, with a fluid internal organization, takes the place of the specialist. This change in the character of the technical division of labor prefigures a deeper shift in the relation of production to science.

The seemingly superficial characteristics of the confined knowledge economy, studied at the level of management and production engineering, turn out to be not so shallow after all. To be fully achieved, they demand more consequential changes. Such changes suggest the existence of a repressed transformative potential.

To achieve an economy-wide presence, rather than remaining arrested within insular vanguards, the knowledge economy would have to make good on powers that are now only a distant promise. To make good on this promise, the advanced productive practice would have to spread throughout the economy: its dissemination and its radicalization are inseparably connected.

3.

The Deep Structure of the Knowledge Economy: Relaxing or Reversing the Constraint of Diminishing Marginal Returns

I now turn from surface to depth: to three features of experimentalist, knowledge-intensive production that it reveals only as it develops and spreads. So long as the knowledge economy remains quarantined within the fringes that it now occupies, it hides its nature. We must infer its potential from the fragmentary evidence supplied by its present insular form.

The first such deeper characteristic is the promise of relaxing or even reversing the constraint of diminishing marginal returns: the decreasing return in output at the margin to successive commitments of any one factor or input in production when the other factors or inputs are held constant. Beyond a certain point, the productivity of successive increments to the input or factor begins to decline. No feature of economic life enjoys a better claim to being considered a universal and timeless law of economic life than this constraint.

To understand the significance of this law and of its possible modification or supersession, it is best to begin by distinguishing it from another idea for which it is sometimes mistaken: returns to scale. The concept of returns to scale refers to the relation between two quantities. The first quantity is the increase or decrease in factors or inputs committed to the production of a good or service, when all inputs or factors are increased or decreased in the same proportion. The second quantity is the resulting rise or decline in output, registered over the long term. Returns are constant when output rises or falls proportionately to the increase or decrease of inputs committed to the production of a good or service.

Returns to scale are normally assumed to be constant. However, any number of circumstances can and do lead to increasing or diminishing returns to scale. A larger factory, in which all inputs have been increased in the same proportion, can be either more or less efficient than a smaller one. The occurrence of constant returns to scale has never been deservedly regarded as a law-like regularity of economic life. It is at best a defeasible factual assumption. It holds true only in the absence of any of the countless circumstances that might negate it, including beneficial or prejudicial interactions among the inputs or factors of production. In this sense it is like constant motion in Newtonian mechanics. It is nevertheless a useful concept because like so much of established economic analysis it facilitates revealing simplification.

Many have suggested that the knowledge economy might be associated with increasing returns to scale and have seen cause for the vindication of this conjecture in particular features of this practice of production. Some such suggestions focus on an advantage enjoyed by part of the knowledge economy: the near-zero marginal cost of adding another customer to the user community of a platform business. These proposals fail to explain how other parts of the knowledge economy, with no such advantage, could share in the experience of increasing returns to scale. They are at best claims about a particular segment of the knowledge economy.

Other suggestions emphasize the positive externalities generated by the insights, skills, and staff on which the firms of the knowledge economy depend. These firms are producers as well as consumers of practical knowledge. The goods and services that they sell are rich in the embodiment of such knowledge and are likely to require knowledge-based skills for their effective use. Moreover, the businesses of the knowledge economy can thrive only by creating around themselves a wide penumbra of people, institutions, practices, and ideas conducive to their work.

All this embodied or tacit knowledge represents what economists have called a "non-rivalrous" good: its use by some fails to deplete its use by others except to the extent that the law of intellectual property intervenes to limit access to it, making a non-rivalrous good "excludable." The proliferation of shared tacit knowledge and capabilities in the knowledge economy will not only foster the development of advanced firms and advanced parts of the production system; it will also make it easier for the successful to flourish yet more, widening their lead. It is they who are in the best position (by virtue of their accumulation of intangible skills as well as of tangible resources) to turn the non-rivalrous and non-excludable goods of the knowledge economy to advantage.

However, such positive externalities are hardly a distinct trait of the knowledge economy. They were common as well, and with similar qualifications, in earlier forms of production: for example, in the heyday of mechanized manufacturing and industrial mass production, given the dependence of these previous productive practices on the mechanical inventions of the nineteenth century and on the science, culture, and institutions that supported the inventors.

Even if these conjectures about near-zero marginal cost or positive externalities could adequately differentiate their subject matter—the knowledge economy—without over- or under-inclusion, they would suffer from a more basic failing: they would explain circumstantial departures from a norm—constant returns to scale—that was never more than a convenient and contingent empirical assumption in the first place.

We must look for the revolutionary significance of the knowledge economy for the future of productivity in another quarter: in its potential to relax or reverse what has indeed been as close to an economic law as anything has been—the law of diminishing marginal returns. Keep all the inputs to a process of production constant and increase one of them. The returns in output to the increase of that input will rise and then fall at the margin.

What resists, avoids, and postpones the fall is innovation—conceptual, scientific, technological, organizational, or institutional. However, insofar as innovation consists in a series of discrete episodes, each innovation is equivalent to an input under the law of diminishing returns. The innovation will result in a rise of output, until its potential to stimulate is exhausted and the marginal returns to its more extensive use begin to decline. The law of diminishing marginal returns—the decreasing productivity of successive increments to any one input or factor in production, when the other inputs or factors are held constant—does not contradict constant returns to scale. In fact, that law takes constant returns to scale for granted over the short term to which it applies. And although it is by convention associated with the short rather than the long term, its recurrence has long-term implications of immense significance. To understand them, it is necessary to identify the cause of diminishing marginal returns.

Given how fundamental the constraint of diminishing marginal returns is to our understanding of how an economy works, it is remarkable that there should be so little clarity about its basis. That basis is the episodic or discontinuous character of innovation, aggravated by the dependence of progress in the production system on scientific and technological breakthroughs—themselves episodic—that are external to this system. Innovation is the only force capable of counteracting diminishing marginal returns. If, however, innovation is episodic or discontinuous rather than continuous and perpetual, each innovation will operate as if it were a new input, or a modification of an existing input, subject to the same constraint of diminishing returns at the margin.

Consider the three forms of discontinuity that have been characteristic of the innovations that played a decisive role in the course of earlier advanced practices of production, and in particular of the immediate antecedent to the knowledge economy: industrial mass production and its precursor, mechanized manufacturing. The first is discontinuity in the history of scientific discovery, as the invention of new ways of understanding nature is followed by the organization or normalization of the resulting theories, experiments, and procedures. The second is discontinuity in the application of scientific insight to technological invention, enhanced by the reverse effect of such inventions, especially of scientific equipment, on the practice of science. The third is discontinuity in the use of technology, based on science, by the production system. These overlapping and cumulative discontinuities, combined with the dependence of production on progress external to itself, form the ultimate basis of the constraint of diminishing marginal returns.

The knowledge economy promises to undermine this basis and thus to create the potential to overcome or even reverse the constraint of diminishing marginal returns. The relaxation or reversal of diminishing marginal returns would thus occur for reasons that are both more fundamental and more specific than those that have been invoked in the arguments about why knowledge-dense production might yield increasing returns to scale. One of the deeper traits of the knowledge economy, I argue in the next section, is to recast production on the model of scientific experimentalism, making the way in which we cooperate more like the way in which we imagine and allowing the worker to be the opposite and the complement, rather than the mirror, of his machines.

The advance of science and technology may remain discontinuous. But the experimentalist production characterizing the knowledge economy can translate scientific discovery and technological invention more directly and continuously into productive activity than it ever could before. Moreover, such production ceases to be the passive beneficiary of what the progress of science and technology brings, and becomes itself a source of ceaseless innovation in ideas as well as in practices and products. It can use what science and technology creates more readily, more fully, and more constantly because it has become more like them.

The more innovation becomes perpetual rather than episodic, and the more it arises from within the production system itself as well as from the use of ideas and machines developed outside that system, the greater becomes the prospect of relaxing or even reversing the constraint of diminishing marginal returns. The constraint may loosen or reverse not just with respect to knowledge embodied in technology but also with regard to every input in the process of production, including both labor and capital. The nature and productive potential of each factor and each input are changed by membership in the knowledge economy.

These speculative propositions yield falsifiable hypotheses. We should be able to observe the loosening of the constraint of diminishing marginal returns, and to do so in proportion to the deepening and spread of the knowledge economy. Success or failure in overcoming this constraint is no idle curiosity. It is intimately associated, I argue in this book, with some of our most weighty material and moral interests.

To relax or to overcome the constraint of diminishing marginal returns would mark a momentous shift in the character of production. From the perspective of that change, the economic history of mankind falls into three large periods.

In the first period, corresponding to only the most primitive conditions, the decisive constraint on economic growth was the size of the surplus over current consumption: what Marx called primitive accumulation. Both Smith and Marx believed that it continued to be the overriding limit to growth in the economies of their own time, their chief object of study. For Marx, the leading explanation of the class character of society, and therefore also of the treatment of labor under capitalism as a commodity that can be bought and sold, was the need to ensure the coercive extraction of a surplus. For Smith, the brutalization of the worker under a hierarchical and specialized form of the technical division of labor formed part of the price to be paid for economic progress: a condition for increasing the stock of capital required for future growth.

Smith and Marx were mistaken: already in their day innovation—ideational, technological, organizational, and institutional—rather than the size of the surplus represented the overriding constraint on growth. Britain did not differ from the agrarian-bureaucratic empires of East, South, and West Asia by having a higher level of domestic private and public saving. Historical research has shown that it had a lower level of saving than many of them. It differed from these other societies in its innovations and in the social, cultural, and political background propitious to them.

In a second period of economic evolution, coinciding with almost the whole of history, from the beginnings of civilization to today, the chief constraint on economic growth became the level, the scope, and the pace of innovation, as well as the relation between innovation in the technologies and arrangements of production and innovation in institutions, science, and culture. Innovation in its many forms turned into the primary driver of growth.

Saving became a consequence more than a cause of growth. However, growth, sparked and sustained by innovation, took place under the double aegis of scarcity and diminishing marginal returns. Innovation, albeit many-sided, remained punctuated: it consisted in a series of discontinuous changes in otherwise continuing practices and arrangements. The most important innovations were those that had to do with the ways in which people cooperate and with the transformation of nature or the enlistment of natural forces to our benefit. The design and use of our machines bore the imprint of these two sets of experiments—with nature and with cooperative practices—and of the ways in which we related them to each other.

A third period in economic history begins when innovation loses its punctuated character and the constraint of diminishing marginal returns is relaxed or even reversed. Scarcity and the unequal consequences of different ways of distributing and using scarce resources continue to rank among the most basic features of economic life. Innovation, however, becomes more perpetual than episodic. It becomes internal to the process of production as well as reliant on science and technology imported from outside the production system. The constraint of diminishing marginal returns loosens because good firms begin to resemble good schools, and the development of production to resemble the development of knowledge.

4

The Deep Structure of the Knowledge Economy: Production, Imagination, and Cooperation

Another deep trait of the knowledge economy is the close relation that it establishes between how we work and how the mind develops ideas and makes discoveries. Production has been the transformation of nature and the mobilization of energy in nature with the help of technologies that enhance our powers. Now it becomes more accurate to say that the growth of knowledge becomes the centerpiece of economic activity. New products or assets and new ways of making them are simply the materialization—in goods and services—of our conjectures and experiments.

Something central to economic life seems to be excluded by this characterization: the way in which we work together in production—the cooperative regime or the technical division of labor—and the institutional arrangements, political as well as economic, within which we cooperate. It is not: as we radicalize the central impulse of the knowledge economy, the way in which we work together to achieve practical goals becomes an expression of our imaginative powers. To press further in this direction, it is not enough to change the way in which we work together at the micro level, in the workplace. We must also reshape the institutional arrangements of the economy and of politics so that they allow us to master and to transform, rather than to take for granted, the settled assumptions and arrangements of the market and of the state.

We cannot understand what is at stake in this translation of imagination into cooperation without first forming a view of the two sides of our mental activity. In one aspect, the mind is like an old-time machine, the kind of machine that was central to mechanized manufacturing and industrial mass production. It is modular: it has different parts, associated with distinct areas of the brain (insofar as there are limits to the plasticity of the brain). And it is formulaic: it operates under stable formulas, rules, or algorithms. As a consequence, its actions are also repetitive.

In another aspect, however, the mind is neither modular nor formulaic. It can exploit the plasticity of the brain to base similar powers on different parts of its physical infrastructure. It can freely recombine everything with everything else—the power that we know in mathematics as recursive infinity. It can discard its settled practices or methods and defy its established presuppositions, and go on to make discoveries or develop insights, the adequate practices, methods, and presuppositions of which it makes explicit retrospectively—the power that the poet called negative capability.

This is the aspect of the mind that we name imagination: the mind as anti-machine by contrast to the mind as machine. The mind in its imaginative aspects has two constitutive operations. The first operation is the one that Kant emphasized: distancing. The image is the memory of a perception. The second operation is the one that Kant disregarded: transformative variation. We grasp a phenomenon by projecting or provoking its change in response to certain natural or staged interventions. We understand the phenomenon by subsuming it under a range of adjacent possibles: what it could become, or what we could turn it into. The approximation of production to imagination is the heart of the knowledge economy, and ever more so as it spreads and deepens.

We can explore the affinity between production and imagination in two ways: with regard to the way of organizing work or the technical division of labor, and with respect to the relation between worker and machine. The relative power or preponderance of the mind as machine and the mind as anti-machine or imagination is not determined by the physical structure of the brain. It is shaped by the organization of culture and society, including the arrangements and practices of production. In this sense, the history of politics—if by politics we mean struggle over the shape of our relations to one another—is internal to the history of the mind.

Under the knowledge economy, the way we work together—the technical division of labor—can begin to resemble the workings of the mind as imagination, and to take on each of its features: its nonmodular and nonformulaic traits and, as it develops more fully, its powers of recursive infinity and negative capability. Production can develop by exploiting, thanks to these traits and powers, new products and possibilities of production at the penumbra of the adjacent possible. The less stark the contrast between supervisory and implementing responsibilities or, as a consequence, among specialized jobs of implementation, the better our chances of identifying and realizing such possibilities.

The productive plan is continuously revised by the work team in the course of being carried out. As a result, specialized responsibilities within the team cease to be rigidly distinct. The fixity of the distinctions among them is just the reverse side of the clarity of the contrast between conception and execution.

This view of how the technical division of labor can and should change may seem puzzling when applied to the economy. However, it has a more familiar military application. An infantry brigade organized as a conventional regular force has a command-and-control structure with stark contrasts between commanding officers and commanded soldiers and fixed responsibilities in the field. As a consequence, it may be very limited in its ability to exploit the potential of the military technologies with which it is equipped: the firepower technologies as well as the communication apparatus. And it will be restricted as well in its capacity to regroup and improvise on the battlefield in response to the surprises of combat.

By contrast, an irregular force, adequately trained, skilled, and equipped, will know no such sharp contrasts between battle planning and execution. It will eschew a rigid command-and-control structure. It will assign to lower-level officers and troops a wider margin of discretion to adjust the plan in the light of emergent obstacles and opportunities. And it may require specialists to be generalists as well. If the unit conforms to this ideal, it will have superior operational capabilities, and it will be capable of making better use of firepower and communication kit than the conventional regular force can. It will be able to disperse and regroup in the field and respond to the surprises of circumstance without losing coherence and momentum.

The line of military evolution is for a regular force to gain some of the characteristics of an irregular force without while maintaining its ability to scale up, to receive central (but loose and flexible) direction, and to preserve coherence and momentum in the field. The same should and can happen in the economy. Its occurrence marks progress in the development and spread of the knowledge economy. The way of cooperating at work comes to bear more fully the marks of the imagination.

Now consider how this same idea of production as imagination may be realized in the relation of worker to machine as well as in the technical division of labor. Under earlier advanced productive practices—mechanized manufacturing and its successor, industrial mass production—the worker worked as if he were one of his machines. His movements—in Adam Smith's pin factory or Henry Ford's assembly line—recalled theirs. The parallelism of worker and machine was more than a metaphor or a distant analogy; it was studied and codified by experts in industrial organization such as Frederick Taylor and offered as a practical guide to managers and foremen.

Under earlier advanced practices of production, we see the mind as machine, even in the most mindful expressions of those practices. No wonder, despite the genuflection that classical development economics made to education as one of the fundamentals of economic growth, little by way of education was in fact required of the worker in the age of mechanized manufacturing and industrial mass production. What he needed was a disposition to obey, basic literacy and numeracy, and manual dexterity, especially hand-eye coordination.

The knowledge economy makes possible—and to develop more deeply and widely it requires—a fundamental change in the relation of worker to machine. This change provides another instance of what it means to reshape production on the model of imagination. Here is the principle governing this change, stated in its simplest and most general form, as an overview of the past, present, and future of machines.

Until very recently the point of machines has been to do for us everything that we have learned how to repeat. Call such machines formulaic. The fact that machines operate formulaically might suggest that their greatest value is to allow those who use them to operate nonformulaically. The users of the machines can then reserve their supreme, and in a sense their only, resource—time—to those activities that we have not yet learned to repeat and therefore to encode in a mechanical device.

Such a relation between machines and their users has not, however, taken hold in the course of the history of practices of production. More often, as the example of the relation between machine and worker in mass production suggests, the worker has been made to work as if he were one of his machines, mimicking its repetitious movements, or complementing them by different but comparably formulaic activities. The result has been to shortchange the potential of technology, even of relatively simple and rigid machines, to allow their users to put to them to best effect by not mimicking them. That potential has been achieved in forms of artisanal or craft production that have been pushed to the margins of the main line of economic history.

The history of practices of production, and of the economies, polities, and cultures in which they are embedded, has overshadowed the evolution of machines and shaped the technical division of labor. Up to now, the idea that the most effective way to use a machine is to work as not a machine, as anti-machine, nonformulaically or nonalgorithmically, has remained a mere speculative possibility.

The advent of the knowledge economy, even in its present insular and relatively superficial form, has been accompanied by the development of machines that challenge our received understanding and use of machines. It has done so especially in the most revolutionary area of technological innovation, now known as artificial intelligence and machine learning. There are two basic ways to understand the machines developed so far in the early history of the knowledge economy.

On one understanding, the machines of the knowledge economy are just higher-order formulaic devices. We do more than encode in them the formulas and algorithms of a limited set of operations, with dedicated uses. We endow them with meta-formulas and algorithms, or higher-order rules of inference, that allow them to infer new movements from example and experience and to change their first-order algorithms and formulas accordingly. We can even build into these machines an element of randomness, to extend the range of experience and example to which they respond in adjusting their procedures.

On an alternative understanding, what these machines are beginning to do is not just formulaic activity of a higher order. They can bypass general rules of inference altogether. We can best understand such extra-formulaic machine functioning as the acquisition of adaptive operational capabilities: from the simplest—how to turn a door knob—to the more complex—how to drive a vehicle safely. Such capabilities develop in the context of the physical performance of tasks.

Under this second understanding of the most advanced machines, what we see as the higher-order rules of inference is simply the retrospective description of an adaptive evolutionary ascent that never needed such rules or at least never needed to make them explicit. The ascent up the ladder of such capabilities resembles the progression studied in Piaget's cognitive psychology: the abstract follows the concrete; the conceptual, the operational. There is a pragmatic residue resisting formulaic reduction or expression.

The meta-formulaic and the operational understandings of this new stage in the history of machines, the stage that begins with the knowledge economy and that we now call artificial intelligence and machine learning, are alternative philosophical accounts of an emergent novelty. We do not have, at least not yet, a reliable basis on which to choose between them. The time may soon come when the rise up the ladder of machine capabilities progresses to a point beyond which it becomes clear that we can no longer treat the two accounts as equivalent or complementary.

Regardless of how we ultimately come to characterize this new stage in the history of technology, something fundamental has already changed in the relation of people to machines. It was possible to organize mass production in a way that cast the worker as an alter ego of his machine, even though that approach squandered the full potential of even those earlier, relatively primitive technologies. However, it is not possible to make the workers of the knowledge economy, even in its present quarantined and truncated form, shadows of their machines. The machines can be much better than human workers could ever be at some things. But the people who use these machines have something that no machine can have: the power to imagine.

The movement from the formulaic to the metaformulaic or post-formulaic is not a movement that enables machines—any machine, even in principle—to embody what I earlier called the second side of the mind: the imagination. The hallmark of the imagination is its negative capability: the ability of the mind to distance itself from a phenomenon or state of affairs and then to subsume it under a range of transformative variations; to cast aside its settled methods and defy its present presuppositions the better to see something that it could not see before, and then retrospectively to develop the methods and formulate the presuppositions that make sense of an insight that could not previously have been generated. Imagination is not about facility. It is about vision. Machines cannot even in principle have this transgressive and visionary power. It is a power rooted in the most fundamental attribute of our humanity: our transcendence over all the finite determinations of our existence, our inability to be contained within the conceptual and social worlds that we build and inhabit.

The most effective use of these machines is their use by workers who do not work and think as if they were machines. The combination of the machine and the anti-machine—that is to say, the worker—is much more powerful than the worker or the machine alone. What we cannot do is to make the machine a seat of imagination, with the power to defy the lower- and higher-order rules that we gave it, and to make sense retrospectively of the discoveries achieved through such defiance. As we improve the machine, appearing to diminish its distance from us, and even to exceed us in certain respects, such as computational power, we run ahead of the machine. Like Achilles in his race against the tortoise, a tortoise of our own creation, in the race that matters most the machine can never catch up with us.

This change in the relation of worker to machine responds to a moral as well as to a material interest of ours. It signals a world in which the worker and the machine diverge, even as the machine does more of what we used to do. Many have raised the specter of machines eventually taking most jobs. I will later argue that under a radicalized, economy-wide form of the knowledge economy, we have reason to expect that the character of work will change but its quantity will not diminish—an argument entirely consistent with the orthodox economic rejection of "lump-sum" theories of labor as objections to technological innovation. The true danger is the inverse one: that the preponderant part of the labor force will remain condemned much longer than it needs to be to do work that machines could execute. Under an economy that develops by respecting our powers, no one should have to do what can be done by a machine.

However, this potential is unlikely to be realized, except in episodic and fragmentary ways, unless we change the institutional arrangements of the market economy. The institutional reshaping of the market order in a particular direction, discussed later in this book, is one of the chief requirements for the deepening and dissemination of the knowledge economy. An element of that change deserves early mention in this account of the relation between worker and machine. So long as economically dependent wage labor, bought and sold under the form of contract, remains the predominant form of free labor, the relation between worker and machine that the knowledge economy favors and requires will tend to be suppressed or contained. The stake of those who organize production, in the name of property, in maximizing managerial discretion inhibits the achievement of this potential. Those power interests oppose revolutionary change in the relation of worker to machine outside a small and insular world of elite workers and technologists.

The completion of the change of the relation of worker to machine requires that wage labor gradually give way, as nineteenth-century liberals and socialists wanted and expected, to the higher forms of free labor: self-employment and cooperation. We shall later see what that nineteenth-century ideal would mean when translated into twenty-first-century realities and possibilities.

5

The Deep Structure of the Knowledge Economy: Trust, Discretion, and the Moral Culture of Production

A mark of the knowledge economy is its tendency to change the moral culture of production, heightening the level of trust and discretion required and allowed in the work of production, enhancing our willingness and ability to cooperate, and moderating the conflict, characteristic of all social life, between cooperation and innovation.

Mechanized manufacturing and industrial mass production, like the types of market order within which they flourished, demand only a modicum of trust. The social theorists of the late nineteenth and early twentieth centuries (such as Max Weber and Georg Simmel) had emphasized the moral presuppositions of the "capitalist" economies of their day. Central to these presuppositions was overcoming the sharp contrast, typical of earlier forms of social and economic life, between the distrust shown to outsiders and the high level of reciprocal trust shared by insiders bound by ties of blood and culture. The market economy could then be understood as a form of cooperation among strangers that is unnecessary when there is high trust and impossible when there is no trust. It depends upon a moderate level of trust—low trust—generalized among strangers.

The classical nineteenth-century law of contract, with its focus on the instantaneous bilateral executory promise and its relegation of continuing relationships to the periphery of contract law, developed this vision as legal rule and doctrine. So did the unified property right, an invention of the nineteenth century, joining, as if they naturally belonged together, a range of powers with regard to things and vesting them in the same right holder, the owner. Unified property became more than just one right among many; it served as the exemplary form of any right.

Within the strict, clear-cut boundaries of his entitlement, the owner was free to do as he pleased, with minimal regard for the interests of others. The accumulation of property became an alternative to the demands of solidarity. Such was a law of things suitable to a society that placed its bet on universalizing low trust among strangers.

With its emphasis on hierarchical specialization, legitimated in the name of property, mass production, like the mechanized manufacturing that it succeeded, reserved significant discretion to those who, as the representatives of capital, oversaw the process of production. By minimizing the area of discretionary maneuver allowed to the individual worker or the work team, it also limited the need to trust the wage laborer or to rely on trust among workers.

In such an economic world, the tension between the imperatives of cooperation and innovation remained acute. Every innovation requires people to cooperate: to develop the innovation as well as to implement it. But every innovation—whether it is technological, organizational, institutional, or conceptual—threatens to shake the established cooperative regime. It does so by arousing uncertainty about the future of the rights and expectations embedded in every such regime. It therefore triggers struggle among the affected groups over how the innovation will influence their relative positions.

We can improve the cooperative regime through initiatives that diminish the tension between the need to cooperate and the need to innovate. For example, we can ensure to each worker a set of universal, portable safeguards against economic insecurity and a series of capability-enhancing economic and educational endowments. We can do so while simultaneously increasing opportunities to innovate in the arrangements as well as in the technologies of production.

The knowledge-intensive advanced practice of production thrives on continuous rather than merely episodic innovation. Consequently, it needs more than generalized low trust. Its subversion of the sharp contrast between responsibilities to supervise and to implement and its ambivalence toward rigid specialization call for wider discretion and greater trust, not just from within a cadre of bosses and supervisors but among rank-and-file workers. It resists the assignment of cooperation and competition to distinct domains of activity, and confides instead in cooperative competition—the fluid mixture of cooperation and competition—within as well as among firms.

These remarks suggest that among the bases of the knowledge economy is an accumulation of social capital—a density of association—and a softening of the tension between the disposition to cooperate and the need to innovate. I argue later in this book that an institutional reshaping of the market economy—of the arrangements of economic decentralization—ranks among the chief conditions for the advancement of an inclusive vanguardism. Another requirement is change in the character of education. But education and institutions are not everything in economic growth or in the deepening and spread of the most advanced practice of production.

The ability to cooperate plays a major independent role. Where does it come from? Must we take its relative strength as an immutable given, or can we influence its evolution? Some countries have tried many institutional frameworks for the economy and failed with all of them. Other countries have proved themselves able maintain a high level of cooperation while changing—if not by a commitment to institutional experimentation, then by force of national emergency—their economic institutions.

In the Second World War, the United States cast aside, under the pressure of necessity, many of the forms of economic organization that were supposedly sacrosanct in the national political culture and ran the economy by methods that were anathema to that culture. Yet the disposition to cooperate across class lines, if not across racial lines, remained. The practical results were spectacular. The combination of a massive mobilization of physical, financial, and human resources with bold—and untheorized—institutional innovation allowed GDP to double in four years—a result unlike any that had ever been seen, before or after, in American history. In war, as in peace, the level of social capital and the disposition and ability to cooperate remained key to worldly success, whether military or economic. In pretending to be something that they were not—a classless society—Americans were inhibited over the long term in attacking the entrenched inequalities that prevented them from taking their cooperative practices to a yet higher level. Nevertheless, their self-deception during wartime may have served them well in the short term by inducing them to cooperate across class lines that they were unwilling or unable to see.

The moral background to the knowledge economy is not just a circumstance that is either present or absent, and in either event beyond the reach of deliberate action and programmatic intent. Where this background is missing, collective action can create it.

6.

The Confinement of the Knowledge Economy: The Fact and the Riddle

Throughout the world the knowledge economy remains restricted to insular vanguards: advanced manufacturing, knowledge-intensive services (often associated with advanced manufacturing), and precision, scientific agriculture. Even as the knowledge economy has lost its exclusive association with industry, it has remained, in each sector, a fringe.

It is true that the boundary separating the knowledge economy from the rest of the production system always remains porous. There is leakage into a penumbra of surrounding economic activity and capability that softens the contrast between the vanguard and the rest. Many forces contribute to such leakage.

Promotion of the knowledge-intensive products and services sold by the businesses of the knowledge economy requires propagation of the skills needed to use them. The technologies and practices of the knowledge economy develop through their extension to new lines of production and new areas of consumption by a process of analogy and generalization familiar in the history of science. Governments anxious to emulate foreign vanguards, as well as to promote their own, learn open-ended and experiment-friendly approaches to regulation that favor diffusion of the knowledge economy around its porous periphery.

Given these prompts to dissemination, it is all the more remarkable that the knowledge economy has continued to be largely confined to the fringes in which it thrives, and consequently as well to be arrested in the expression of its deepest attributes and the achievement of its larger potential. In some ways, as I argue in the next section, its confinement has increased rather than diminished. Leakage has not turned out to be the first step to an economy-wide uplift of productive practices and capabilities.

It might nevertheless become one—part of the point of departure for a movement toward a deepened and widespread form of the new style of production. It will not serve as such a starting point spontaneously. We must act to create this alternative future. To create this future we must be able to imagine it. Until then an inclusive knowledge economy remains a distant goal.

The relative insularity of the knowledge economy has now persisted for so long that we may be tempted to think of this quarantine as natural, as if it called for no further elucidation. There is, however, nothing natural about it. Mechanized manufacturing and industrial mass production rapidly influenced the transformation of every part of the economy, with the notable exception of traditional small business, which was prevented by its limited scale from assimilating the scale-dependent technologies and procedures of mass production.

Unlike earlier advanced practices of production, the knowledge economy has no intrinsic bond to any particular sector. Its ability, supported by its characteristic technologies, to produce goods and services at almost any scale would open to it the world of small business, if that world did not remain largely inaccessible to it for other reasons. Yet its confinement to insular vanguards has stubbornly persisted.

Not only has the knowledge economy escaped a restriction to industry without avoiding insularity, it has also overcome an exclusive connection with the richest economies in the world without as a result moving toward an economy-wide presence in any of them. In the heyday of mass production, the axis of the international division of labor, as well as the core topic of analysis in the theory of international commerce, was trade between capital-intensive and labor-intensive economies. The most advanced practice—industrial mass production—was headquartered in the richest economies. More primitive, labor-intensive production remained dominant in the rest, the vast periphery of the developing world.

The emergence of the new advanced practice of production has coincided with a striking change in the world division of labor. The new productive vanguard has gained a foothold in all the major economies of the world: in the major developing countries (such as China, India, and Brazil) as well as in the richest economies. The advanced parts of these economies are, to a greater or lesser extent, in direct communion with one another, exchanging people, procedures, and ideas as well as technologies and resources. Indeed, the network of these vanguards has a better claim than any other set of economic agents and forces to be regarded as the commanding force in the global economy. By comparison, international finance is a sideshow.

The worldwide presence of the knowledge economy, manifest in the changed international division of labor, only deepens the puzzle presented by its arrest within the fringes to which it is now confined. It is present in every major economy as well as in every part of each of them. Yet it remains the prerogative of an elite. In this situation, forces related to the confinement of the knowledge economy work in concert to favor economic stagnation and aggravate economic inequality. Slowdown in the growth of productivity and deepening of economic inequality are the price paid for the insularity of the knowledge economy.

7

Pseudo-Vanguardism and Hyper-Insularity

We must be careful not to mistake the insular knowledge economy for what I shall call pseudo-vanguardism: the existence of a wide range of firms that make use of the technologies we most often associate with the emergent vanguard, especially its information and communication technologies—without otherwise mastering and deploying the new most advanced practice of production: either its superficial features, which I described at the level of management or production engineering, or the deeper traits that it reveals as it develops and spreads.

The most common form of pseudo-vanguardism has been the adoption of digital technologies to manage complex information—for example, the information with which a mega-retailer like Walmart must deal. By managing information more effectively, such businesses have been able to develop efficiency-enhancing and capital-sparing practices such as the "just-in-time" replenishment of inventory. Their large scale has given them a decisive advantage in dealing with the fixed cost of the required technological apparatus. Their successful use of that apparatus has in turn helped them grow yet larger, consolidating their market position. Yet none of these initiatives has converted such megafirms into exponents of the knowledge economy. Pseudo-vanguardism makes the knowledge-intensive advanced practice of production seem more widespread than it is.

The real knowledge economy remains stuck in a narrow circle. The incentives to accumulate profit and amass market power reinforce the narrowness. The large global firms that dominate the knowledge economy find ways to factor out parts of their process of production that can be routinized or even commodified. They assign these routinized parts to businesses staffed largely by semi-skilled labor, using the methods of conventional mass production, in parts of the world remote from headquarters. Some advanced firms are even "fabless," ridding themselves to the greatest extent possible of the ownership of large productive units (factories) and of any commitment to the stable workforce that such units traditionally require.

Genuine vanguardism remains restricted to a small inner circle of entrepreneurs, managers, and technicians—an elite of capital and of knowledge—disengaged from the social entanglements of mass production. Subcontracting, or more generally decentralized networks of contractual arrangements, with other firms in other countries, under different rules, often replaces the incorporation of labor in the home country into the work of the knowledge economy. The lion's share of the gains goes as capital appreciation to the shareholders of the firms operating at the commanding heights of the insular knowledge economy. It goes as well to an elite of super-skilled workers and managers in the form of quasi-wage benefits such as stock options.

The counterpart to the illusory dissemination of the advanced practice by pseudo-vanguardism then becomes the hyper-insularity of the genuine vanguardism. The advanced firm retreats into an arm's-length contractual relation with the companies that fabricate whatever material goods it may have to sell. For example, a few thousand people in California arrange for hundreds of thousands of people in China to execute the routinized parts of their production plan.

Hyper-insular vanguardism is the authentic but miniaturized form of the knowledge economy. Pseudo-vanguardism is its illusory long shadow. The coexistence of hyper-insular vanguardism with pseudo-vanguardism is accompanied by two developments that are more than coincidentally connected and that bring increasing economic stagnation and inequality in their train. The first development is the decisive position acquired by global oligopolies. The second development is the abandonment of an increasing portion of the labor force in the richest as well as in developing economies to precarious employment. The result is to increase the advantage of capital over labor in the contest for a share of national income, except for labor performed in the shrinking recesses of hyper-insular vanguardism and of the entrepreneurial and technological elite controlling it.

Both pseudo-vanguardism (the Walmarts of the world) and hyper-insular vanguardism (the Alphabets and Qualcomms of the world) are marked by vast scale and imperfect competition. For both, the megafirm enjoys an advantage over its smaller rivals in the ability to bear profitably the fixed costs of investment in the most advanced equipment. Moreover, the hyper-insular advanced firms—the genuine embodiment of the vanguard of the knowledge economy—enjoy three additional advantages in avoiding effective competition. They are limited, tangible expressions of what makes the knowledge economy different: the primacy in its work of ideas, capabilities, and networks that are intangible, although supported by physical infrastructure and accessed by material devices.

The first prompt to expansion and oligopoly consists in the platform effects of businesses such as the megafirms of the hyper-insular knowledge economy. These businesses learn to sell products only as part of platforms or ecosystems, associating a multitude of goods and services with one another. The larger the platform and the greater the number of participants, the stronger the appeal to new customers because the options the platform offers to its participants are more varied and complete.

The second prompt is the edge the megafirms of the genuine knowledge economy enjoy in attracting technical talent. To the material benefits resulting from work for a vast enterprise, holding vast amounts of liquid capital, is added the appeal of working for a firm that operates at the frontier of technological evolution. To be successful, such firms must resemble laboratories; the young technologist or technological entrepreneur, the young scientist, wants to be part of a team in touch with the most advanced work in his field.

The third prompt may at first seem to be prosaic and shallow despite its importance: the engagement with products and services the reproduction of which for the next consumer may have near zero marginal cost. An instantaneous and nearly costless operation may suffice to introduce him to the platform and give him access to many of its products and services. He may pay nevertheless for something that imposes no additional cost on the mega firm and by increasing the size of the user population may help make the platform proportionately more valuable to other users in the future. This seemingly trivial trait signi-fies more than it at first appears to mean; it results from a practice of production in which knowledge and the communities of users that it makes possible counts for more than material products and processes. All such processes and products are subject to costs, attritions, and degradations that are pervasive in nature. All belong to a world in which the constraint of diminishing marginal returns continues to rule.

8.

Precarious Employment

The other development accompanying the duo of pseudo-vanguardism and hyper-insular vanguardism is the degeneration, to the disadvantage of labor, of the relation between labor and capital. One of the most constant doctrines of economics has been that returns to labor—the real wage—cannot sustainably increase above the rise in productivity. This dogma contains a residue of truth: a mandated rise in the returns to labor is likely to be undone by inflation. Aside from this qualification, however, we know that the dogma must be false: for if we compare economies at comparable levels of development and control for different factor endowments (notably population density and wealth in natural resources), we find that there is wide disparity in the division of national income between labor and capital. How could this disparity have arisen in the first place?

The cause of this divergence lies in the legally defined institutional arrangements that either strengthen or weaken labor in its relation to capital and shape the terms on which labor can be recruited for production. Economic growth requires repeated breakthroughs of the constraints on both supply and demand. The most long-lasting and effective ways of breaking through the constraints on demand are those that influence the primary distribution of economic advantage rather than trying to correct that distribution after the fact through progressive taxation and redistributive social entitlements. Among the arrangements that shape the primary distribution of economic advantage are those that set the legal status of labor vis-à-vis capital (contract, corporate, and labor law) and those that define the terms of decentralized access to the resources and opportunities of production (the property regime).

A way of empowering or disempowering labor in its relation to capital is secure if it has a basis in the most advanced practice of production. The approaches to organizing and representing labor that prevailed in the course of the twentieth century enjoyed such a foundation. The predominant arrangement for organizing and representing labor in the rich North Atlantic world and its outposts was the contractualist or collective bargaining labor-law regime: collective bargaining was designed to shore up the reality of contract in the unequal setting of the employment relation thanks to the "countervailing power" with which it endowed organized labor. In Latin America, an alternative, corporatist labor law emerged: workers (in the formal, legal economy that often accounted for half or less of the labor force) were automatically unionized according to their sector, under the tutelage of the ministry of labor. Both the contractualist and the corporatist regimes had as their economic setting industrial mass production, with its characteristic gathering of a stable labor force in well-defined productive units (factories and others) under the aegis of business corporations.

The emergence of the insular knowledge economy has not replaced mass production with a similarly economy-wide advanced productive practice. The development of this new vanguard forms part of a reality in which traditional mass production is declining and its commitment to a stable labor force is left without solid economic support. Corporations scour the world for cheaper labor, more dispensable labor commitments, and tax favors (labor and tax arbitrage). The insular knowledge economy and the nonvanguard firms around the world to which it assigns work through unstable contractual arrangements help undermine the economic base on which both the contractualist and the corporatist labor-law regimes rested.

What has seemed to be the natural form for the representation and protection of labor may turn out in retrospect to be only a relatively brief interlude between two periods in which labor was organized primarily by means of decentralized contractual arrangements, without economic security or citizenship. Before industrial mass production and the contractualist and corporatist labor-law regimes, it was the putting-out system, which Marx described in the early parts of *Capital*. Now, in the wake of the decline of mass production and of its overtaking by a new advanced but exclusionary practice of production—the insular or hyper-insular vanguardism of the established form of the knowledge economy—another putting-out system has arisen on a global scale. Many mass-production jobs are subcontracted to low-wage firms in poorer countries. Others are replaced by insecure piecework and temporary employment, especially in services. In the absence of an alternative legal regime for the

representation and protection of labor and, more fundamentally, of initiatives that would move toward an inclusive vanguardism, labor becomes defenseless and its share
in national income declines.

The responses offered so far to the developments accompanying the emergence of hyper-insular vanguardism and
of pseudo-vanguardism—the control of both by oligopolies
and the relegation of a growing part of the labor force to
precarious employment—are grossly inadequate. They
would work only if they were swept up into a larger and
broader transformation. To this day, such a change has not
even been imagined, much less implemented.

Consider the appeal to antitrust law as an answer to the
domination of the knowledge economy by oligopolies,
surrounded by a periphery of unthreatening start-ups. The
factual conditions that would allow for the application of
antitrust law are often missing: for example, suppression of
competition in a well-identified market for certain products and with measurable effect on product pricing.
Suppose antitrust law were amended or developed to deal
with the ways in which the megafirms of the knowledge
economy suppress competition. The revised law would be
unlikely to reverse the combined and cumulative forces,
enumerated earlier in this section, that have given a small
number of global firms a decisive advantage in combining
hyper-insularity with oligopoly. Such revisions of antitrust
law would work only as part of more far-reaching changes
in the institutional and legal architecture of the market
economy.

Moreover, the breakup of platform companies risks
destroying much of their economic and social value,

which is tied to the number of people that they bring together in a single community of users. Instead of breaking them up into smaller firms, organizing less inclusive networks, we may decide to preserve them but to subject them to new forms of governance. For example, independent trusts, established by law, with representatives of civil society might have powers to direct or restrain them, thus qualifying the rights of shareholders and the authority of managers.

The efficacy of either antitrust or governance initiatives is likely to depend on more far-reaching innovations in economic institutions. Such innovations would begin by broadening access to the means of engagement in the knowledge economy: capital, advanced technology, and advanced practice. They would continue in the creation of new forms of partnership between governments and emergent firms as well as of cooperative competition among them. And they would result in pluralistic experimentation with the basic property regime: the ways in which, and the terms on which, people can deploy the accumulated capital of society and make use of productive resources and opportunities. It is a sequence exemplifying the legal and institutional element in the advancement of an inclusive vanguardism, as the successor to the present confined form of the knowledge economy.

In similar spirit, consider "flexsecurity"—the Scandinavian experiment in the development of security-preserving safeguards and capability enhancing endowments that are vested in every worker-citizen, independent of holding any particular job and that are therefore universally portable.

The safeguards and endowments move with the worker from job to job. Some such arrangement must form part of any effective response to employment insecurity under the new realities of production. Its wider adoption would demonstrate that flexibility and security need not be inversely related. The result would exemplify an aspect of a regime attenuating the tension between innovation and cooperation. However, like antitrust with respect to the cartelization of the knowledge economy, it can provide no more than a fragment of such a response.

The broader antidote of which it would form part would have to create another labor-law regime alongside established labor law, which was made for an economy that is ceasing to exist. Such a regime would be designed to ensure that labor-market flexibility not serve as a euphemism for unmitigated economic insecurity.

One of its principles would be the adoption of a sliding scale. The more that precarious labor is organized and represented, with the help of the communication technologies and practices of the knowledge economy, the less need there is for direct legal intervention in the employment relation to protect the precarious worker. Conversely, the less precarious labor is organized and represented, the stronger becomes the case for such direct legal protection.

Another principle, developing the content of such protection, would be for the law to require the price neutrality of the choice between stable and part-time or task-oriented employment for similar work: the contract worker would have to be paid at least as much as the stable employee for analogous labor. The aim would be to guarantee that the flexibility required by the practices and relations of the knowledge economy not serve as a pretext or as a disguise for the cheapening of labor and the reduction of its share in national income.

In later stages of the evolution of this alternative labor-law regime, changes in labor law would give new life and new meaning to the belief, shared by nineteenth-century socialists and liberals (from Karl Marx to John Stuart Mill), that economically dependent wage labor is a defective and transitory form of free labor, retaining some of the features of serfdom and slavery. It ought to give way in the future to the higher forms of free labor—self-employment and cooperation. Their relegation to subordinate or peripheral status only began to appear natural and necessary in the latter nineteenth century. The institutional arrangements and the private law of an inclusive variant of the knowledge economy would revive and reinterpret that nineteenth-century ideal, reshaping it in the light of twenty-first-century conditions.

An inclusive vanguardism is the only adequate answer to the menacing developments that accompany the rise of the knowledge economy in its present globalized but insular form.

9.

The Confinement of the Knowledge Economy: Consequences for Economic Stagnation and Inequality

The confinement of the knowledge economy has momentous consequences. Today it has become the single most important cause of both economic stagnation and economic inequality. To overcome this confinement by moving in the direction of an inclusive vanguardism would reignite accelerated growth and begin redressing the sources of extreme inequality in the hierarchical segmentation of the economy.

The most advanced practice of production may not be the most efficient in its early manifestations. However, it is the one with the best chance of reaching the frontier of productivity and staying at it. To acquiesce in its confinement to fringes within each sector of the economy is to deny the vast majority of workers and firms the level of productivity that our technical achievements have already made possible but that our economic and social arrangements have failed to make available to ordinary workers.

Moreover, the most advanced practice of production is historically the one with the greatest power to inspire imitation and change in the rest of the economy. To allow it to remain the prerogative of a technological and entre-preneurial elite is to deprive the rest of the economy of its greatest potential source of direction and inspiration. It is as if we had decoupled the locomotive from the rest of the train. The effect of this failure is all the more startling and demoralizing if—as happens with the knowledge econ-omy—the advanced practice has no intrinsic relation to any particular sector and has in fact gained a foothold in many sectors, though always as fringe.

One of the most significant and least obvious ways in which this confinement contributes to stagnation is by its effect on the vanguard itself, even in those parts of the production system and labor force in which this vanguard-ism thrives. If it is true that a practice of production devel-ops and reveals its potential only as it adapts to a broad range of circumstances, then the insular form of the prac-tice is likely to be misunderstood even by its own agents and beneficiaries. It will be easily mistaken for its most superficial or accidental characteristics, such as those that marked the high-technology industries and regions in which it first appeared. Unlike mass production before it, it will lack an accepted theory or doctrine endowing it with a canonical form and a widely accepted significance. It will be at once fashionable and obscure.

The consequences for inequality are no less significant. The insularity of the knowledge economy, and its relative poverty of jobs, intensify the hierarchical segmentation of the economy. An increasing proportion of wealth is produced by a diminishing part of the labor force. What I have labeled hyper-insularity aggravates this tendency. The job structure associated with mass-production industry and its counterpart in services gets broken up into two pieces.

The larger piece is composed of lower-wage jobs in services rendered in the domestic market and in conventional manufacturing work carried out in countries that offer the cheapest labor and the lowest taxes. Such jobs may offer work in the leftover of declining mass production, remaining viable only at the cost of low returns to labor and a low tax take. Or they may create positions in a variant of standardized manufacturing that has become the sidekick of the megafirms of the knowledge economy, as they learn how to routinize parts of their production process and assign the commoditized parts of their business to dependent companies, often in faraway places. The second piece of the new labor market is the privileged one: the relatively small number of jobs established in the recesses of the genuine and exclusive knowledge economy. In the wake of the continuous decline of mass production and its reduction to leftover or sidekick status, there results what has been described as the "hollowing out of the middle of the job structure."

Progressive taxation and redistributive social entitlements can be effective in moderating inequality generated by the established arrangements of the market economy so long as inequality does not become too extreme. Beyond an ill-defined threshold, structural realities overwhelm corrective measures. Corrective redistribution on either the revenue-raising side of the budget (progressive taxation) or the spending side (redistributive social entitlements and transfers) would need to become massive to compensate for the vast disparities generated by the chasm between the vanguards and the rearguards of production.

Long before it reached that point, corrective redistribution would begin to clash with established economic institutions and incentives and to exact a price in foregone economic growth that would be widely regarded as intolerable. It is one thing for progressive taxation to extend the logic of established arrangements; it is another thing for it to contradict that logic. In this latter, humanizing role, it can make a decisive difference only by going very far toward overturning market-determined outcomes and disorganizing the economy. No wonder that it is almost never allowed to go that far. It is stopped long before then.

The more promising route is to organize a different market economy, one that generates less inequality and more widely distributed stakes, instruments, capabilities, and opportunities in the first place. A high tax take will be needed to fund the state that such a reconstruction of the market order requires: a state that is able to invest in people and their capabilities as well as in the physical infrastructure of production, to sponsor the costliest and most radical technological innovations, and to partner, to that end, with emergent or established private enterprise in return for stakes in their future.

Similar reasoning applies to the other side of corrective redistribution: social entitlements and transfers. Such measures will always be insufficient to compensate for the stark inequalities rooted in chasms between the advanced and backward parts of the production system. Their more compelling and effective use is of a different order: they can do a great deal to form people who are unafraid and capable enough to become the agents of a changed economy. In this respect, we would continue in a different register the most important accomplishment of twentieth-century social democracy: its massive investment in people and their capabilities, paradoxically financed by the regressive and indirect taxation of consumption. We would do so while overcoming the greatest limitations of historical social democracy: its abandonment of innovation in the institutional arrangements of the market and of democracy, its lack of a progressive approach to the supply side of the economy, its single-minded emphasis on corrective redistribution rather than on change in the arrangements determining the primary distribution of economic advantage, and its subordination of the ideal of shared empowerment in both economic and political life to attempts to humanize a largely untransformed economic regime.

If our aim is to connect the logic of economic growth with a movement toward inclusion and greater equality of opportunities, capabilities, and stakes, the best way to do so is not through after-the-fact correction—the effort to attenuate the unequal effects of an economic order that we despair of reimagining and reshaping. It is to reimagine and to reshape that order. Instead of the fantastical wholesale substitution of the established economic regime by an imaginary, readymade alternative, we need cumulative structural change, undertaken piece by piece and step by step. In such an endeavor, no task is more important than to confront the inequality-aggravating effects of the present confinement of the most advanced practice of production.

Three propositions summarize and begin to explain the comparative fiscal experience of the richest economies of today with respect to inequality. Although these principles are relatively simple and straightforward and supported by long and dense experience across a wide array of different circumstances, they remain largely alien to the discourse of social democracy and social liberalism—the most characteristic projects of governing elites in the North Atlantic countries today.

The first proposition is that initiatives influencing the institutional arrangements that organize access to economic and educational opportunity and capability, and consequently shape the primary distribution of advantage, are what matters most to the future of inequality. They overshadow everything that can be accomplished by way of after-the-fact redistribution through progressive taxation and redistributive entitlements and transfers. Today the chief locus of the contest over the anchoring of inequality in economic arrangements is the struggle over the future of the most advanced, knowledge-deep practice of production: whether it is to remain confined to insular vanguards, as the province of an entrepreneurial and technological elite, or to set its mark on the entire economy.

The most admired form of economic and social organization has been Scandinavian social democracy. If the world could vote, it would vote to become Sweden—an imaginary Sweden rather than the real one. Many associate the humanization of the market order through compensatory redistribution with the imaginary Sweden, and forget that this humanization through social and economic rights was preceded by many decades of class and ideological warfare over the interests of the moneyed classes and the power of the state. This conflict ended in a settlement between the dynastic plutocracy of the country and the regulatory and redistributive commitments of the social-democratic humanizers. The world would like to enjoy the epilogue without having to undergo the preceding narrative. And it fails to recognize the limits of an agenda that has as its overriding ambition to reconcile European-style social protection and American-style economic flexibility within the limits of a barely adjusted version of the inherited organization of the market economy and of democratic politics.

Such a program is unable to provide an adequate antidote to inequalities rooted in the division of the production system among the insular knowledge economy, the unsalvageable mass-production industries, and traditional, retrograde small business. It cannot supply a sufficient basis for social cohesion once ethnic and cultural heterogeneity has exposed the weakness of money transfers organized by the state to supply the missing social cement. Moreover, it is powerless to create a political life under democracy that can dispense with economic or military crisis as the enabling condition of structural change.

The second proposition to infer from contemporary fiscal experience with regard to inequality is that taxation and social spending do perform an important albeit subsidiary role. However, at least in the short to medium term, what counts most in the regime for taxing and spending is not the progressive profile of taxation. It is the aggregate level of the tax take and how it is spent. What we lose by way of progressive redistribution on the revenue-raising side of the budget we may gain in double on the spending side.

In many contemporary societies, the indirect and regressive taxation of consumption, especially through the flat-rate comprehensive value-added tax (VAT), may be the best way to sustain such a high tax take, which can be and has been used to finance a high level of social entitlements. The reason is uncomplicated. It is nevertheless too paradoxical to be palatable to the conventional progressive discourse. The VAT is by definition the tax most neutral in its bearing on relative prices. So long as it is left untainted by exceptions subversive of its neutrality, it takes for the government a constant proportion of the value of the transformation of every input into every output. Consequently, VAT makes it possible to raise the greatest amount of revenue with the least amount of economic disturbance. Much of that revenue can then go to redistributive social investment, more than compensating for what has been foregone, by way of equalizing redistribution, on the revenue-raising side the budget. Would-be progressives in contemporary politics most often fail to recognize the primacy of structural change over compensatory redistribution. They commonly prefer progressive pieties to transformative effects, even in their favored terrain of tax-and-transfer.

The third proposition is that over the long term we can achieve a redistributive effect, subsidiary to both structural change (the first proposition) and the maintenance of a high tax take even if reliant on regressive taxation (the second proposition) so long as we design the tax system with an understanding of the relationship of tax instruments to redistributive goals. The primary proper target of progressive taxation is the hierarchy of standards of living, generated by the income and wealth that each individual takes out of the resources of society and spends on himself. The tax instrument best suited to hit this target is a tax on individual consumption.

Such a tax (most fully studied by Keynes's disciple Nicholas Kaldor and sometimes known as the Kaldor tax) would fall on a steeply progressive scale on the difference between the total income of each individual (including returns to capital) and what he spends on himself. There are no technical difficulties in the administration of such a tax other than the difficulties of the conventional tax on personal income. It enjoys, however, two advantages over the personal income tax. It hits the target of unequal standards of living directly, whereas the income tax is both a blunt and a hybrid instrument. Moreover, it allows for a top marginal rate that can be as high as political will and power make possible; 100 percent ceases to be the upper limit.

Beneath a certain threshold of personal expenditure, the individual would receive rather than pay. Above that threshold he would pay on a rising scale. And above a certain level of luxury living, for every dollar that he spends on himself, he would have to give several dollars to the state. If progressives were both clear-sighted and sincere in their devotion to the redistributive use of taxation, this is the tax that they would prefer. They would prefer it at the third level of their thinking about the redress of inequality, after they had first assured the priority of structural change over compensatory redistribution, and then, with respect to the latter, recognized the priority of the aggregate level of the tax take and of the way it is spent over the progressive profile of the tax system.

The secondary target of progressive taxation is the exercise of economic power, achieved through the accumulation of wealth and its hereditary transmission at death or by gifts *inter vivos*. This target is secondary not because the goal is any less important but because there is less prospect of reaching it though taxation. A tax on wealth would have to be massive, and cause major economic disruption, before it could hope significantly to alter the present distribution of assets. Its best chance is to influence that distribution over time through the taxation of actual or anticipated inheritance. For the exercise of economic power, even more than for the hierarchy of standards of living, institutional innovation in the arrangements of the economy, to the end of broadening access to opportunities and capabilities, trumps by far anything that we can hope to achieve after-the-fact through progressive taxation and social spending. The most important such innovations are those that broaden access to the most advanced practice of production.

Progressive redistribution by taxation and social spending has often been used as a surrogate for structural change. Structural change has in turn been represented as the revolutionary substitution of one indivisible economic system for another. Such a substitution is ordinarily inaccessible in politics and policy (except in the extraordinary circumstance of a great crisis). If it were accessible, it would be feared as too dangerous.

One of the aims of this book is to help bring the conception of structural change down to earth. The changes that we most need are the piecemeal and gradual but nevertheless cumulative and ultimately radical innova-tions that would take us from a confined to an inclusive knowledge economy. The exploration of these changes forms the principal subject matter of the remainder of this book.

The confinement of the knowledge economy to insular vanguards undermines economic growth and aggravates economic inequality. No adequate response to these prob-lems of stagnation and inequality can fail to address their sources in the gap between the vanguards and the rest. The loss of opportunity visited on us by the insular vanguard-ism of today is not, however, limited to the costs of economic stagnation and to the inequities of economic disadvantage. We are made smaller as well as poorer and more unequal by our failure to give economy-wide form to our most advanced practice of production.

The core of the knowledge economy at its deepest level is the tie that it seeks and needs to establish between imag-ination and cooperation: the change of our cooperative practices into a way of imagining together in our produc-tive activities. The turn of cooperation into a mode of imagination is barely perceptible in the established forms of the advanced practice of production; failure to dissemi-nate this practice results in failure to deepen it.

However, even in its existence under quarantine, the knowledge economy already showers on its participants an array of moral as well as material benefits: the taste of an experience of work that gives wider room to the creative impulse. By laying in the prosaic realities of production a basis for the predominance of the mind as imagination over the mind as a formulaic and modular machine, it has the potential to make us bigger. Of all the insults of the confined vanguardism that has been established, none is more consequential than the denial of this experience to the vast majority of people, even in the richest and most educated societies.

Later parts of this book explore the requirements of an inclusive vanguardism—the reliance on an education that is dialectical in its approach to the received body of knowledge and cooperative in its social setting; the remaking of the moral culture of production to permit and demand higher trust and greater discretion; and the reshaping of the institutional architecture and of the legal regime of the market order. These requirements are more than means to the end of disseminating the most advanced practice of production in every part of the economy and to deepen it by doing so. They are also ways of raising our experience to a higher plane of scope, capability, and intensity, a plane on which we cease to be the hapless puppets of the social worlds that we build and inhabit, and gain instead the power to turn the tables on these worlds. We have reason to rebel against insular vanguardism not only because it impoverishes and divides us but also because it belittles us.

10.

The Confinement of the Knowledge Economy: The Beginning of an Explanation

Why does experimentalist, knowledge-intensive production remain restricted to the advanced fringes of each sector of the economy, with the consequences for economic productivity and growth as well as for economic inequality and disempowerment that I have discussed? The answer to this question has immense practical importance. It bears directly on our understanding of what we can do to advance the cause of an economy-wide form of the most advanced practice of production.

The best way to begin to answer the question is to consider by contrast what happened in the relation of the previous most advanced practice—industrial mass production, sometimes also called Fordist mass production—to the economy as a whole. We can describe this earlier most advanced practice as the large-scale production of standardized goods and services by rigid machines and production processes, on the basis of semi-skilled labor and highly specialized and hierarchical work relations. It assembled a stable labor force in large productive units under the aegis of big or medium-sized businesses. It required of its workers repetitious moves mirroring the moves of the rigid machines with which they worked. It affirmed a stark division between supervisory and implementing responsibilities at work as well as among jobs in executing productive plans.

Mass production was made possible by a series of technological, organizational, institutional, and conceptual innovations: for example, steam or combustion engines, machine-cutting lathes, and metal-making converters; a way of organizing the technical division of labor modeled on the military organizations of the historical period in which it arose; and a legal framework allowing managers to exercise, in the name of property, wide discretionary authority over the labor force. Innovations were understood and organized as episodes precipitated by events in technological invention and scientific discovery, in law and politics, or even in finance, that were external to the routines of production. They promised to raise productivity and threatened to disrupt established ways of doing business. As a result, they triggered conflict over the consequent distribution of gains and losses to different segments of the labor force as well as to different sets of asset owners.

From the outset and throughout its history, mass production has been chiefly associated with one sector of the economy: industry. Moreover, it flourished principally in the richest economies of the world. From there, it spread to developing countries seeking to gain their own place on the frontier of economic growth. Despite its close connection with industry, mass production has served as a model influencing every sector. These two forms of expansion, from the central to the developing economies and from manufacturing to other sectors, may at first seem to have little to do with each other. In fact, mass production was susceptible to diffusion across sectors for the same reason that it invited geographical dissemination.

Mass production is formulaic. It thrives on repetition and standardization, not just of products but also of processes: of ways of working and even of ways of thinking. It reserves innovation or disruption to an external or in any event a superior authority: the manager acting in the name of the owners even if the owner is the state. The requirements to establish it and to operate it may be exacting but they are also limited. Like its methods, they are stereotypical.

The educational requirements of mass production for ordinary workers are minimal: willingness to follow orders and to understand oral or written instructions, combined with whatever physical competence the specialized task assigned to the worker may presuppose. The job-specific and machine-specific skills needed to use rigid, dedicated machines have been the traditional concern of vocational training in the age of mass production. They place few or no demands on the acquisition of higher-order capabilities.

As a result, the skill and mechanical repertoire of mass production resembles a kit that can be taken from one place to another, no matter how different. In that far-away place it can be counted on reliably to generate the same results once its modest operational requirements are met. It is this characteristic that explained the appeal of the core recommendation of classical development economics: shift people and resources from every other part of the economy (especially agriculture) to mass-production industry. A boost to productivity and growth would, according to the doctrine, regularly follow.

The consequence, long studied and prized by development economics (but now no longer reliable, for which reasons that I shall discuss), is the "unconditional convergence" to higher productivity and growth that resulted from heeding the message of giving more, by way of people, resources, and political support, to manufacturing, even at the cost of raiding the rest of the economy. The convergence to higher growth was regarded as unconditional in the sense that it has recurred across a wide range of countries and circumstances. It was limited, according to the orthodoxy of development economics, only by the ultimate constraints of education and institutions. Even these constraints, however, turned out to be both modest and elastic, given how little was required of education for mass production to flourish and how thin its institutional requirements seemed to be: security in private property and a state with the planning and regulatory powers and cadres that allowed government to receive and follow the advice of development economists.

The same stereotypical character of mass production helps explain how the model of mass production could be influential in the redirection of parts of the economy remote from manufacturing, even in a period of economic history when the distinctions among sectors of the economy retained greater force than they do today.

In services the model of mass production merged into what Max Weber had described as "bureaucratic rationalization" whenever service provision was standardized and conducted on large scale. These conditions were met more often in public services than in the private service economy. Thus, the dominant model of public services to this day has been an administrative Fordism: the provision of standardized low-quality services by the bureaucratic apparatus of the state. Low quality means of lower quality than the analogous services that people with money can buy on the market. The sole alternative to administrative Fordism has been the privatization of such services by their assignment to profit-driven firms.

The persistence of administrative Fordism has drawn renewed life from the absence of the most promising alternative: the cooperative, not-for-profit, and experimental provision of public services by independent civil society, equipped to partner with the state. The state would ensure a universal minimum to all—the floor—and push forward, at the frontier of administrative practice, the development of the costliest and most complex services—the ceiling. In the broad middle zone between floor and ceiling, the state would prepare, equip, finance, and coordinate independent civil society, acting through civil associations or cooperatives of specialists, to share in the work of building people—which is what public services do. Such an alternative would represent, by contrast to administrative Fordism, the administrative counterpart to the knowledge economy. Like the knowledge economy, it would require institutional innovation—in the organization of the state and of its relation to civil society rather than in the arrangements of production and exchange.

In agriculture, mass production exercised its influence again when scale was combined with standardization of products and processes, as in much of entrepreneurial agribusiness. When farmers, for lack of capital, disposition, or scale, failed to embrace the agricultural equivalent of mass production, the trading companies with which they dealt when they sold their crops often imposed it on them anyway. And the risk unique to agriculture—of the superimposition of price volatility and climate volatility, financial risk and physical risk—pushed them to adopt practices that would satisfy their insurers as well as their buyers.

It would require a different set of arrangements to continue and reinvent in the first part of the twenty-first century what Americans had achieved in the first half of the nineteenth: to establish technologically advanced agriculture on the basis of cooperative competition among farmers and of decentralized partnership between the farmers and local or national government. In the twenty-first century, the new most advanced practice of production appeared on the land as precision, scientific agriculture restricted to a fringe of large-scale agricultural entrepreneurs and their commercial and financial backers.

The knowledge economy has failed to spread, as mass production did, with less apparent reason to do so, for two fundamental reasons. They are closely connected. The first reason is that it is not formulaic: from its relatively superficial features to its deeper attributes, it cannot, as mass production can, be reduced to a stock of readily transportable machines and procedures and easily acquired abilities. It thrives on the disruption of routine and repetition and introduces innovation into the daily habits and arrangements of production. The second reason is that its deepening and spread rest on demanding requirements addressed in the next few sections of this book. Unlike mass production, it is neither stereotypical in its content nor minimalist in its requirements.

Happy historical accidents may sometimes substitute for the fulfillment of these requirements. They may make certain regions, and the social and cultural networks that have developed in them, hospitable to the development of today's insular vanguardism. For example, it has often been observed that pre-Fordist craft production, with its traditions of customized artisanal labor, of apprenticeship, and of dense ties in the local community, generate a setting favorable to the development of the post-Fordist knowledge economy: pre-Fordism favors post-Fordism. And indeed many of the regions where a confined form of the knowledge economy has taken hold, especially among midsized firms, such as Emilia Romagna in Italy, Baden-Württemberg in Germany, and Catalonia in Spain, are places with a long past of craft production.

Wherever such a historical sequence stands in the place of wider structural change, guided by a vision of the unrealized potential of the knowledge economy, the most advanced practice of production will exist only in the socially and geographically restricted way that I have called insular vanguardism. Its agents and beneficiaries will mistake it for its shallow and circumstantial form and remain complicit in its arrested development.

The two traits of the knowledge economy that help explain why, unlike mechanized manufacturing and mass production, it has so far failed to set its mark on the whole production system (except by selling its wares to all but the poorest and least educated—pseudo-vanguardism) are directly related to each other. The knowledge economy has demanding presuppositions because it is not formulaic. It can be nonformulaic because it rests on those presuppositions. The more developed and disseminated it becomes—and its development and diffusion are two aspects of the same changes—the more it comes to depend on those conditions and to progress and spread through their fulfillment.

In the next few sections I discuss three sets of requirements for the dissemination of the knowledge economy: the educational-cognitive, the social-moral, and legal-institutional. The third is the least familiar but the most important; it deserves the closest consideration. I then go on to explore the changes in the culture and consciousness as well as in the political institutions of a democratic society that would favor the fulfillment of these requirements. What emerges from the argument about the requirements and the cultural and political background to their fulfillment is the outline of a program for the advancement of an inclusive vanguardism.

Do not regard such a program as a blueprint or a system. It is a direction, to be understood and undertaken in the spirit of "combined and uneven development." We can advance on any of these fronts more rapidly than on others, as circumstances may allow. But we will then hit against limits that we can breach only by advancing on the other fronts. We refine and revise our understanding of the direction as we go along: each moment in such a trajectory will disclose ambiguities, opportunities, and obstacles that only the surprises of transformative action could have revealed.

As always in a programmatic argument, an understanding of structural change—of how it happens or fails to happen—must inform the proposals. We need not, and ordinarily we will not, represent and develop this understanding in the discourse of comprehensive social and economic theory. We will more often prefer to advance by means of fragmentary, context-bound thinking. But a preference for such thinking over systematic theorizing does not exempt us from the imperative of clarity about structural change.

If we focus on the initial steps by which to move in the chosen direction, our proposals may seem realistic but trivial. If instead we imagine steps many moves ahead, our proposals may appear to be interesting and inspiring only at the cost of being utopian. Almost anything that can be proposed in the present climate of opinion is likely to seem either trivial or utopian. However, it is not the moderation or the extremism of our proposals that matter; it is the trajectory to which they belong, whether they are close to present arrangements or remote from them.

The language of transformative politics regularly prefers to combine the earliest and the most distant steps; it is at once practical and prophetic. It seeks to provide or to evoke down payments, in the realm of the adjacent possible, for the redirection that it seeks, drawing energy from the association of ideals and interests with examples within grasp.

In conceptual work, however, it may be most useful to define and discuss the direction at a middle range between the closest and the most distant steps. The politician and the prophet have reason to avoid the description of initiatives that exceed, but not too much, the reach of the *theres* that we can readily reach from *here*. Such initiatives are likely to be too close to established reality to arouse enthusiasm yet too far away to appear feasible. They have, however, an advantage: they stand a better chance than the early or the remote steps of elucidating the character and difficulties of the direction. They may seduce less and clarify more. In the development of this program for an inclusive vanguardism, it is on the middle range that I now chiefly focus.

11

Making the Knowledge Economy Inclusive: The Cognitive-Educational Requirements

A n inclusive vanguardism is a radicalized vanguard-ism: as it spreads across a wide range of circum-stances, in every sector of the economy and in every part of each sector, the experimentalist, knowledge-intensive practice of production reveals and develops its deepest attributes. Its association of cooperative activity with imagination—and with perpetual innovation—requires a higher order of capabilities from its participants than mass production needs. It therefore also calls for a certain kind of education, both in youth and throughout life.

This style of education crosses the divide between general and technical education; by reforming both of them in the direction that I next describe, it places them on a continuum. My subsequent account of its characteris-tics is therefore meant to apply to vocational training as well as to general education.

In its approach to technical education it must repudiate the model of technical training that the world learned from Germany: one emphasizing the job-specific and machine-specific skills needed to operate the rigid machine tools of the age of mass production and to navigate economies organized around the historical, rigidly separated trades and professions. It must put in the place of that model one giving pride of place to generic, flexible, high-order capabilities.

The numerically controlled machine—the programmable robot or 3D printer—has no narrow, dedicated use, tied to a particular line of production and a defined profession or segment of the labor force. The distinctions between inventing it and reprogramming it, and between reprogramming and using it, have all been relativized. Its operator must have some small part of the powers and the attitudes of its inventors. The ability to take full advantage of artificial intelligence goes farther in the same direction; it calls for a worker who knows how to let the machine best him at formulaic tasks so that he can devote himself to nonformulaic ones.

The technical division of labor, even under the confined forms of the knowledge economy, attenuates the contrast between planning and execution as well as among all specialized work roles. In its more developed forms, the knowledge economy makes both possible and necessary a higher threshold of both trust and discretion for all its participants. It needs its agents to have been educated to exercise such discretion and to deserve such trust. They must be able to share in the work of a type of innovation that is perpetual and internal to the process of production, not episodic and directed from outside that process.

The education of protagonists of an inclusive form of the knowledge economy must exhibit four basic characteristics. These features apply to both general and technical education and to lifelong education as well as to the education of the young. They are important or even vital to the development of the knowledge economy. Their value, however, like the value of the knowledge-intensive practice of production itself, transcends their economic benefits and touches every aspect of life and consciousness in a democratic society.

The first characteristic is that the method of education must give priority to analytic and synthetic capabilities, and more generally to the powers associated with the imagination—the mind as anti-machine—over the mastery of information.

No one can acquire these capabilities in a vacuum of content. Content, however, matters chiefly as the setting for the enhancement of capabilities. Thus, the second trait of this education is that with respect to content it prefers selective depth to encyclopedic superficiality. Engagement in depth, around themes or projects, counts for more, in the development of the requisite capabilities and of the deployment of information in the future, than the memorization of any précis of the encyclopedia.

A third mark of this education is that in its social setting, it affirms cooperation in teaching and learning over the juxtaposition of authoritarianism and individualism that has traditionally characterized the classroom. Teams of students and of teachers within and among schools should be the primary instrument of teaching and learning. There should be a wide range of experiments in cooperative practices, including the teaching of students by other students. The meeting of imagination and cooperation is central to any radicalized version of the knowledge economy. To take hold, it must be presaged by the way in which we teach and learn.

A fourth attribute of this way of teaching and learning is that it be dialectical: that every subject and method be presented from at least two contrasting points of view. Once we abandon the goal of encyclopedic content and come to prefer depth to coverage and development of analytic and synthetic capabilities to the recital and memorization of facts, there is time for such a dialectical approach at every stage of schooling.

The orthodoxies of the university culture naturalize in each field the marriage of method to subject matter, inducing the young to mistake dominant ideas for the way things are. Thus, economics is not the study of the economy; it is the study of a method pioneered by the marginalist economists at the end of the nineteenth century. Any inquiry into the economy conducted by another method is not recognized as economics, and the application of the method to subjects with no direct relation to the activities of production and exchange is treated as if it were economics. Similarly, the historical method, with its implication of the ascendancy of temporal change over immutable regularities, is treated as appropriate to natural history and the life sciences, but banished from fundamental physics despite the discovery of the historical character of the universe.

National curriculums infantilize such academic orthodoxies, expressed by the unwarranted naturalization of marriages between method and subject matter. They project the orthodoxies back to the education of the young. The result is to emasculate the student and to hand him to the higher stages of education prepared for a life of intellectual servility. The dialectical approach to education seeks to immunize the young against this danger. Where the university culture is superficial, it proposes depth and openness. It jumbles up what the system of disciplines and methods keeps apart. It aims to form a different mind: one that refuses to treat radical doubt and intellectual experimentation as the prerogatives of genius and turns them instead into a common possession.

The radicalized knowledge economy demands continuous rather than episodic innovation in arrangements as well as in products and technologies. Democracy requires that politics be able to master the structure of society and to produce structural change without needing crisis—in the form of ruin or war—as the enabling condition of such change. The dialectical approach to education helps form the mind on which both democratic politics and knowledge-intensive production depend.

A larger vision of education animates this agenda. The school must equip every student with the instruments with which both to move within the existing order of society and culture and to resist, transcend, and revise that order. It must recognize in everyone a tongue-tied prophet. It must not allow itself to be turned into the instrument of either the family or the state. The family says to the student: become like me. The state says to him: serve me. The school must make it possible to reject these messages. It must be the voice of the future.

But how is that voice to speak, and who can claim to speak it? Education must be arranged in such a way that none of the tangible powers of present society be able to reduce the school to its service. Teachers and students must have the political, legal, and financial means to contain the influence of the state and of the family, and to open up a space in which students and teachers can deal experimentally with the central tension in education under democracy: the conflict between preparing people to act on the basis of the present arrangements and assumptions and equipping them to defy those assumptions and arrangements.

Stated as fleshless and intransigent abstractions, these professions of educational faith may seem otherworldly. Yet they carry into our views of education impulses that are central to the knowledge economy in its radicalized and disseminated form as well as to the political regime most favorable to such an economy, which I will call high-energy democracy. By reshaping our cooperative practices on the model of our imaginative activities and by making innovation perpetual rather than episodic, the knowledge economy requires that its participants have minds that can increasingly dispense with the contrast between doing things and changing the framework of arrangements and assumptions within which we do them. A high-energy democracy moves in the same direction by laying the basis for a form of political life in which structural change no longer requires ruin or war as its enabling condition. Under such a regime the whole order of social life becomes susceptible, in fact as well as in theory, to contest and experiment.

In any contemporary society the most significant obstacle to changing education in this direction is likely to be the absence of a pedagogic vanguard: thousands of teachers and educational activists committed to develop such a program and to make it work. This program cannot advance if it lives only in the minds of a small coterie of visionaries, politicians, and civil servants.

Moreover, in any country that is large, unequal, and federal in structure (or combining a unitary state with significant devolution), the reform and the reformers must be able to rely on an institutional setting reconciling national standards of investment and quality with the local management of the schools. The key principle to observe is that the quality of the education that a young person receives must not depend on the happenstance of where or to whom it is born. Three instruments are needed: a national system for assessing school performance and discovering what works best, a mechanism to redistribute resources and staff from richer places to poorer places (preventing the exclusive dependence of the schools on local finance), and a procedure for corrective intervention. If a local school system falls persistently below the minimum acceptable level of efficacy, central and local government (or the three levels of the federation under a federal regime) must act together to take command of the local failing schools, assign their management to independent administrators and specialists, fix them, and return them fixed. In the absence of such a procedure, the principle of ensuring that educational opportunity not be hostage to the accidents of birth remains dishonored.

I earlier remarked that nothing in the physical structure of the brain determines the relative power of the two sides of the mind: the side ruled by tropisms that can be represented retrospectively as algorithms and formulas, and the side, which we call the imagination, that dispenses with formulas, takes methods at a discount, and overrides its own settled presuppositions. The plasticity of the brain may help enable the imagination but cannot account for its work. It is the organization of society and of culture that shapes the relative prominence of these two aspects of our mental experience. The history of politics is in this sense internal to the history of mind.

The part of the history of politics and of the mind that concerns me here is the potential of the knowledge economy. I have argued that its deepening and its economy-wide dissemination are two aspects of the same phenomenon: if it seems to spread without radicalizing, as happens under the aegis of what I have called pseudo-vanguardism, that is only because it is not the new advanced practice of production that is being propagated. Only its products—devices and services—are then being sold. The capabilities and attitudes acquired in the course of this superficial extension are just those required for the limited use of the products that have been bought.

The radicalized and widespread knowledge economy is both the cause and the consequence of a change in our mental life as well as in our economic activities. Under inclusive vanguardism, the mind as machine must lose territory to the mind as imagination. Change in our economic arrangements and practices of production is not enough to ensure this shift. The shift also requires renewal in the character, conception, and method of education.

12

Making the Knowledge Economy Inclusive: The Social–Moral Requirements

Inclusive vanguardism requires a change in the moral culture of production. This change consists in a way of working that sustains a heightening of the level of trust and discretion required of all who share in the work. It lies as well in an enhancement of our cooperative practices with distinctive and demanding characteristics.

The central issue is whether this shift in the moral basis of production is a feature of practice and consciousness that we can deliberately develop rather than a given of culture that we are powerless to influence. It can and should form part of a program for the advancement of inclusive vanguardism: the moral culture of the deepened and disseminated knowledge economy need not remain a fate beyond the reach of transformative action; it can be a collective creation. We cannot hope to strengthen it, however, unless we understand its composition and requirements.

Within the workplace an approach to the division of labor based on command and control closes the space for discretion and substitutes power and monitoring for trust. The repetitious character of work, mimicking the operations of rigid machines, leaves the specialized implementers of productive tasks little occasion to redefine the plan that they are charged with executing. An implicit term of the employment contract—the contractual form of wage labor—is that all residual discretion to direct the process of production is reserved to managers appointed by owners, within the restraints of law and collective bargaining.

In the established arrangements of the market economy, the central legal devices organizing decentralized access to productive resources and opportunities are the unified property right (a legal invention of the nineteenth century) and its counterpart in contract law, the bilateral executory promise—an arm's-length deal, fully specifying the terms of a bargain that is exhausted in a single performance. Together, the unified property right and the bilateral executory contract set up a regime starkly separating an area of privileged discretion, in which the right holder need take almost no account of the interests of other people—the zone of his entitlements—and a surrounding field in which he becomes subject to the claims of others.

In such a world, a realm of arm's-length dealings and nearly unchecked self-interest stands in stark contrast to every part of social life in which social interdependence is paramount: the family, the community, the church. We accumulate things the better not to depend on people, and reserve incomplete agreements to the parts of social life—family and community—in which we allow power, exchange, and allegiance unashamedly to mix.

The deepening and spread of the knowledge economy require a different moral culture and help develop that culture; an inclusive vanguardism is both cause and consequence of the moral setting in which it thrives. However, it can never be the sufficient architect of its own moral basis. That basis must also be the result of deliberate action.

Consider the requisite change in the moral climate of economic life from the two complementary perspectives invoked at the beginning of this section: the raising of the bar of trust and discretion and the strengthening and refinement of our disposition to cooperate.

The heightening of trust and discretion in turn develop by softening the contrast between the planning of productive tasks and their execution, as the plan is revised in the course of being implemented, and by relativizing the difference between the parts of our activity that we assign to competition and those that we reserve to cooperation.

Remember the military analogy: as the knowledge economy develops, the work group must come to resemble an irregular force more than a conventional one. It is one thing, however, for an irregular military force—such as a special operations unit—to operate as an elite, auxiliary element within a larger army that continues to act in the traditional way. It is another, and more ambitious, agenda for the entire regular force to acquire little by little the characteristics of the irregular one. To do so, it must reconcile the ability to scale up and to maintain central direction with the extreme flexibility and mobility of the elite units. It is just this task, not yet accomplished by any army, that the agents of a radicalized and widespread knowledge economy must achieve.

It is a change that is unlikely to go beyond its initial stages until there is progress with regard to the cognitive-educational and the legal-institutional requirements of inclusive vanguardism. To flourish, a knowledge economy for the many needs an education of the type that I earlier described. It depends as well on legal and institutional innovations in the institutional and legal arrangements of the market economy that multiply the forms of decentralized access to productive resources and opportunities. So long as finance continues to serve itself more than to serve the productive agenda of society, increasing its share of the gains while diminishing its contribution to the creation of new assets in new ways, the control of major productive assets will continue to be exercised by those who command the disposition of large-scale pools of free-floating capital. So long as we fail to innovate in the means for decentralized access to productive resources, which is to say in the property regime, economically dependent wage labor will survive as the predominant form of free labor. Under these conditions, the necessary change in the moral culture of production can begin but it cannot continue and develop. A change in consciousness and in practice will gain force by connection with a change in structure.

The need to raise the level of trust and discretion is simply the most pressing implication of a more general imperative: to strengthen and to refine the capacity to cooperate, which includes both a disposition and a skill. The willingness and the ability to cooperate are no mere creatures of institutional design, although institutions have a bearing on them. Cooperative capability is an independent factor, of immense consequence, in social and economic life. If it is weak, no institutional regime will work as its authors intended it to work. If it is strong, it may produce its beneficial effects through the medium of different institutional regimes.

Early European social theorists, like Machiavelli, Harrington, Montesquieu, and Vico, were aware of both its importance and its irreducibility to institutional choice. They studied it under names such as "spirit" and "virtue." Subsequent classical social theory (as in Marx, Durkheim, Weber, and Simmel) lacked the equipment with which to recognize its importance and to explore its variations and effects. To speak of a cooperative capability persisting across the history of different regimes is to suppose what this theoretical tradition denies: that there is always more in us than there is in the regimes we build and inhabit. In the later history of social science, after this tradition had been redefined as a closed and dead canon, cooperation reappeared as a topic in the diminished and anodyne form of "social capital"—the relative density of our social bonds.

By a cooperative regime I mean a cluster of habitual forms of interaction, the attitudes, skills, and assumptions associated with them, and the institutional and legal arrangements that they take for granted and accept as their template. From the standpoint of its contribution to a practice of production, and especially to the development of the most advanced practice, there are two overriding standards by which to judge the fecundity of a cooperative regime for output and productivity.

The first standard is the extent to which a cooperative regime taps the talent and energy of the widest number of economic agents and broadens their access to productive resources and opportunities. Some ways of organizing a market economy may be better than others at reaching certain groups, or types of individuals. Some ways reach more people, in more ways, than others. However, given that a market economy has no single natural and necessary form, even an approach to economic organization that seems to afford more people more access and opportunity than all its visible rivals do will remain flawed. It too will tilt the scales of opportunity and access. The sole reliable solution will be for there to be no single legal architecture of the market—including no single regime of property and contract—in any given market economy. Alternative institutionalized approaches to the decentralization of economic initiative will then coexist experimentally within the same market order.

The second standard by which to judge the improvement of a cooperative regime is that it moderate the tension between the requirements of cooperation and innovation. This achievement is important for any approach to cooperation; it has extraordinary significance for a practice of production that seeks to render innovation perpetual. Any development of our practical powers—of which economic growth and the increase in productivity are only instances—requires that we both cooperate and innovate. Innovation requires cooperation: to formulate it, to implement it, and to develop it, whether the innovation is technological, organizational, institutional, or even conceptual. However, every innovation disturbs the established cooperative regime. It does so by threatening the vested rights and the settled expectations of the groups that participate in that regime—segments of the labor force vis-à-vis one another, or workers, employers, and investors in relation to one other. Every innovation generates uncertainty about the effects of its adoption on relative group positions.

Even a technological innovation has indeterminate consequences not just for the society at large but also for the participants in the process of production. The pre-shaping of these consequences begins in the conception and design of machines, in the form of assumptions about how, by whom, and in what manner they are to be used. Indeed, the best way to think about technology is to understand it as the materialization of a connection between our experiments in the transformation of nature, deploying natural forces and matter to our benefit, and our experiments in the reconstruction of cooperative regimes. A feature marking one productive practice as more advanced than another is that it goes further in connecting these two sets of experiments. Then we can bring to each set of experiments the lessons learned in performing the other one.

The imperatives of cooperation and of innovation both depend on each other and contradict each other. They do not, however, contradict each other uniformly. One cooperative regime differs from another by diminishing the conflict between the requirements of cooperation and innovation, even if we can never hope to dissolve the tension. For example, one regime may dissociate the way in which it gives people safeguards against insecurity from measures that inhibit the innovative recombination of people, machines, and other resources. It may deepen the plasticity of social arrangements while preventing this plasticity from resulting in fear and haplessness.

The two vantage points from which I have addressed the moral basis of the knowledge economy—the raising of the level of trust and discretion allowed and required in our productive activities and the improvement of the cooperative regime by the twin standards that I have described—are of unequal importance and generality. The former represents an expression or an aspect of the latter: a cooperative regime that taps the talents and energies of more people and goes further toward reconciling the need to innovate with the need to cooperate will be one that does better than previous regimes at empowering its participants (discretion). It will also be one that requires them to accept a higher degree of reciprocal vulnerability and uncertainty (trust). It will do so against the background of strong protections and endowments that enable people to remain unafraid in the midst of change.

At the center of this vision of the moral conditions of the developed and widespread knowledge economy is a view denying any stark, unqualified contradiction between what we give to Caesar (the realm of self-interested exchange, in which our relations to others are merely instrumental) and what we give to God (the domain of our experiments in solidarity in which, to use Kant's phrase, we see and treat others as ends in themselves). It is not that our self-interest and ambition become any less unruly and ferocious, or that we can impart to the economy the hope of interpersonal engagement that we are accustomed to reserve to the most intimate sphere of life. It is rather that our stake in the development of our productive powers through the rise and spread of the knowledge economy requires change in the moral culture of production.

The question to which this discussion of the moral basis of the knowledge economy leads is whether we can develop this basis through collective action or institutional innovation translated into law. We can indeed; it is not just a cultural fate that we are powerless to influence. We can identify initiatives that in their cumulative and combined effect contribute to such a change.

I place these initiatives under three headings: those that strengthen the capacity to cooperate outside the economy, with repercussions for economic activity; those that soften the tension between the imperatives of cooperation and of innovation and move toward a cooperative regime hospitable to perpetual innovation; and those that increase the chance that the regime of cooperation—and the institutional arrangements standing behind them—give productive opportunity to the broadest range of economic agents in the most varied ways. The first set of initiatives goes to changes in culture and politics; the second, to the relation between security and flexibility in the labor market; the third, to the way a market economy is organized and shapes, through contract and property rights, the terms of decentralized economic initiative.

Strengthening cooperative capability outside the economy will result in strengthening it within the economy: the overall tenor of daily experience will teach the lessons that people take most to heart. Here are three examples of social innovations that work to reinforce both the ability and the willingness to cooperate, not least by facing and surmounting the obstacles to cooperation in each of the areas to which these examples refer. Each of them helps achieve independently valuable social goals. Each of them also changes the moral experience of economic agents outside the economy with foreseeable repercussions on the moral climate of economic activity.

One example is the cooperative character of education. If we conduct teaching and learning cooperatively, through teamwork between teachers and students, among as well as within schools, and prompt the young to share active responsibility for one another's education, the impulse to cooperate will have roots in the early formation of the individual. Another example is the engagement of civil society, alongside the state, in the not-for-profit provision of public services, in the spirit of the attempt that I earlier described to reach beyond the limits of administrative Fordism. Civil society outside the state can build both people and itself through the cooperative provision of health and education (by means of cooperatives of service providers or of social organizations), complementing rather than displacing the action of the state, and the self-organization of the community, together with the police, in the suppression of violence. Yet another example is the generalization of the principle that every able-bodied adult should take care of others outside his own family as well as holding a position within the production system. Voluntary or mandatory social service should establish the policy and legal framework for this effort to give tangible expression to social solidarity.

How can we develop arrangements that exploit the reciprocal dependence of the imperatives of cooperation and innovation while moderating the conflict between them? The most important feature of such institutional arrangements is that they accomplish something that appears to be, but is not in fact, a contradiction in terms:

that the safeguards of the individual against economic insecurity be designed to equip him with capability-enhancing endowments (both economic and educational) while throwing economic institutions and practices open to challenge and reconstruction to the greatest feasible degree.

Before considering this task in its institutional form, think of it first in its psychological expression. To be useful to himself and to others, the individual must not live in constant and paralyzing fear. Yet he must also be shocked out of conformity: his habitual forms of action must be challenged by change all around him. The quality of his lived experience must intensify, as it sheds its tropisms: habit and conformity are enemies to vitality.

He must be secure and capable. Yet his security and capability must not be acquired and maintained at the cost of freezing social and economic life. On the contrary, they must be the reverse side of his willingness, once secured in a haven of vital protected interests and powers, to see society and culture around him change.

For the individual, part of the solution to this problem lies in a resistance to his own character—the rigidified, habitual form of his self, of his way of being—that rescues him from dying, by steps, within this petrified version of the personality. For the society and its economic order, however, the solution consists in disentangling the assurance of security and capability from the imposition of constraints on the plasticity of social and economic life: its openness to challenge and change. Some measure of interference with plasticity is unavoidable. The rights and benefits ensuring security and capability must be relatively stable: they must be removed from the agenda of short-term politics. It can never be more than a relative removal: the content and scope of these guarantees and endowments as well as the means by which best to develop them always remain contestable.

We take something out of the agenda of political contest and social experiment the better to enlarge that agenda: to put more things more deeply in question. We do not allow the sense of individual and collective identity, and therefore of safety against the insecurities that innovations bring with them, to be invested in the preservation of the established forms of social and economic life. We develop the safeguards and the endowments of the individual worker and citizen not to prevent change—of the economy, the society, and even the self—but to enhance our creative and transformative power.

A small, initial instance of movement in this direction is the contemporary set of reforms in historical social democracy that have been labeled flexsecurity: the redefinition of work-related rights and benefits to make them fully portable rather than dependent on holding a particular job. Its proponents conceived it as part of what has become the dominant project today of governing elites in the richest countries: the reconciliation of European levels of social protection with American commitment to economic flexibility. We may, however, think of it instead as a moment and a fragment in the broader endeavor of developing cooperative regimes that internalize the impulse permanently to innovate.

Once we redefine the goal in this way, we must pursue it by multiple means through two parallel sets of initiatives.

One set will develop the package of safeguards and endowments: for example, by giving everyone at birth a social inheritance, a stake in the productive assets of society, that he can monetize and draw upon at turning points in his life. Another set will reorganize both economic and political life in ways rendering the established structure of society more susceptible to piecemeal but cumulative reconstruction, even when change cannot count on the opportunity provided by crisis. The two sets of initiatives are likely to clash at particular moments, or with respect to particular issues. The same vision informs them: there is no overall or lasting contradiction between them.

No single organization of the market economy can do justice to everyone's potential or to the value of every line of economic experimentation. No system of impersonal right can be neutral among substantive conceptions of the good. It can nevertheless put the accessible and valuable aims of openness to contradiction and to correction in place of the illusory and dangerous ideal of neutrality. So, too, the ideal of a decentralized economy lacks a natural form: there is no definitive, all-purpose version of a market order, not even a natural system of private property and contract.

The particular approach to property and contract that developed in purest and most intransigent form in the nineteenth century and that has never since lost its central place in private law and legal doctrine is not a natural legal language in which we can think every economic thought worth thinking, and with which we can establish every economic initiative worth establishing. It is a limiting language, made all the more restrictive by the pretense of neutrality and elasticity invoked in its favor.

Some ways of organizing the market are better than others. They may be better because they afford more decentralized access to the resources and opportunities of production in more ways. They may also be better because they allow for invention and experiment in the institutional and legal shaping of economic decentralization.

These two varieties of superiority in the organization of a market are connected. The greater the room for diversity and experiment in organizing the means of decentralized economic initiative, and consequently as well in the regimes of property and contract, the less likely it becomes that the organization of the market will give an entrenched advantage to certain groups, classes, types of economic agents, and lines of productive activity. Each property regime—which is to say, each way of organizing decentralized access to productive resources and opportunities—will tend to favor a different cast of agents and interests. The best guarantee of openness is not to sanctify one version of the market as the natural and necessary one, in the manner of market fundamentalism. It is to allow many versions—many regimes of property and contract—to coexist experimentally in the same market economy and in the same body of law.

The consequence of entrenching one version of the market, usually to the benefit of a few, will be to cast justified suspicion on the cultivation of common purpose—in the firm or in the economy and the nation as a whole—that is vital to strengthening the will and the ability to cooperate. Always the threshold issue for an ideal of solidarity is to identify and justify its structural assumptions: what it takes for granted by way of how to organize an economy rich in opportunities for decentralized initiative.

The bane of commitments to solidarity has been to serve as a halo conferred on an institutional framework that is left unchanged and even unrecognized. The imperative to cooperate becomes a prompt to muffle conflict. So it happened, for example, in European politics and in the social teaching of the Catholic Church, especially in the period between the two great wars of the twentieth century: the evocation of cooperation between workers and owners in firms and whole sectors, under the eyes of a state anxious to convert class conflict into national cohesion and social conformity, served as a weapon against labor militancy and socialist agitation. The outcome was then, and would be now, to weaken rather than to strengthen the moral and social basis on which a developed and widespread knowledge economy must rest.

The sole acceptable form of the improvement of the cooperative regime is one that avoids this misdirection. To do so, it must resist entrapment in a unique and exclusive way of organizing the market economy. To succeed in such resistance, it must move in a direction allowing alternative ways of structuring decentralized economic initiative and decentralized access to productive resources and opportunities to coexist experimentally within the same market economy. What this means for the institutional reconstruction of the market I now discuss.

13.

Making the Knowledge Economy Inclusive: The Legal-Institutional Requirements

Inclusive vanguardism requires cumulative revision of the institutional arrangements of the market economy. To overcome the legacy of insular vanguardism—stagnation, inequality, and belittlement—it is not enough to regulate the market more intensively or to go further than we have gone up to now in redressing economic inequalities through progressive taxation and redistributive social entitlements and transfers. We must reshape the institutional arrangements that define the market economy. We can and should refuse to accept the market order on a take-it-or-leave-it basis, as if we could choose only between having more or less market, and more or less governmental intervention in that market. We can choose to build a different market economy.

This thesis contradicts a characteristic assumption of much of practical economics and of thinking about economic policy. According to this assumption, economic failures result from localized flaws in market competition (such as the rigidity of the price of labor, or asymmetrical information, or a disturbance in the relation of agents to their principals) or in the regulatory response to such market failures. The conception of an institutional and legal reshaping of the market order contradicts a history of modern ideological controversy that is built around the contrast, or the balance to be struck, between market and state.

Similarly, this conception is incompatible with the idea, common to much of classical social theory, that history witnesses the evolution of a closed list of social and economic regimes (such as "capitalism"), each of them an indivisible system. As a consequence, it also contradicts the view that change achieved through politics must be either revolutionary (replacing one system by another) or reformist (managing or humanizing a system) in the manner of today's institutionally conservative social democrats or social liberals.

Instead, it affirms that structural change is almost always fragmentary and piecemeal. Radical ends can be achieved—and ordinarily are—by gradual means, so long as movement persists in a certain direction. To envision such a direction, and to translate it into a sequence of steps, is the work of both transformative practice and programmatic thought.

In this spirit and on the basis of these working assumptions, imagine three stages in the development of the institutional and legal foundations of the inclusive knowledge economy. Institutional arrangements live as law. Law is the institutional form of the life of a people. Our interests and ideals are always nailed to the cross of our institutions and practices. Law is the site of this crucifixion. It has a dual nature: as the repository of detailed institutional arrangements and as the expression of an understanding of the interests and ideals that those arrangements are designed to serve.

The task of the first stage of legal and institutional innovation is twofold. It must seek to broaden access to the resources and opportunities of production, especially in favor of emerging firms that are candidate carriers of the new most advanced practice of production. It must also help organize the process by which we can discover experimentally the best path to an inclusive vanguardism.

Access to capital, to advanced technology as well as to the practices and capabilities with which it is associated, to a labor force equipped with the requisite skills, and to domestic and international markets (not just as sources of demand but also as sources of a benchmark to meet) are all necessary. It is not enough, however, to provide these forms of access separately. The most important and difficult task is to orchestrate them, designing them in such a way that they reach beyond the familiar protagonists of the insular knowledge economy (e.g., high-technology industry) to every part of the production system.

Private venture capital has historically performed this role but only on a small scale (small in proportion to total financial activity) and with a focus on a relatively exclusive cast of start-ups steeped in the culture of the present, confined form of the knowledge economy. Government may need to help create multiple, independent, and competitive entities, supported at the outset by public funding, that undertake this work on behalf of a broader pool of economic agents—the next wave of firms that seek to share in the work of the knowledge economy—and with a longer time horizon. It may do so under market rules (although as part of an effort to develop new kinds of markets) and by taking equity stakes, as venture capitalists do, in the entrepreneurial activity. The aim should be to make this quasi venture capital self-financing as soon as possible.

As the instances and agents of the knowledge economy widen, the range of pertinent experience of the firms themselves becomes richer. There is no reliable, established body of knowledge about how in detail to adapt the technologies and practices of the existing, contained form of the knowledge economy to people and firms who have thus far remained untouched by its practices and culture even when they buy and use some of its products. An important aim in this initial stage of institutional reconstruction of the market economy is therefore to find out, through the experience of the beneficiaries of broadened access, what practices work best and then to disseminate them.

That too is a task of the state. But like the orchestration of access to each of the resources that successful production requires, it is not a task suitable for implementation by a conventional administrative apparatus acting under central direction to formulate a unified set of rules and policies. It is work best discharged by a level of support centers intermediate between the government and the client firms, by analogy to the system of agricultural extension that was first developed in the United States and other countries in the course of the nineteenth century.

At a second stage, there would begin to emerge an alternative institutional and legal architecture of the market economy. Unlike the changes in the first stage, these initiatives would have explicit implications for the overall organization of the market economy; they would do more than introduce into the established market regime new agents and practices. Unlike the changes in the third stage, they would stop short of radical innovation in the mechanisms of decentralized access to productive resources and therefore in the content of private law. Consider these second-stage changes on two axes: the vertical axis of relations between governments and firms and the horizontal axis of relations among firms.

There have long been two models of relations between government and business on offer in the world: the American model of arm's-length regulation of business by government and the northeast Asian model of formulation of unitary trade and industrial policy, imposed top down by a governmental bureaucracy. Neither of these models is adequate to the development of institutions that can provide a basis for deepening and spreading the knowledge economy.

The first model—arm's-length regulation—takes the arrangements of the established market regime for granted. That an inclusive vanguardism does not arise naturally under those arrangements is shown by its failure to develop in any contemporary economy. We can attribute that failure to the absence of other conditions, such as the requisite form of education or a moral culture favorable to higher trust and discretion. Then, however, we must ask what economic institutions will either inhibit or encourage these other changes. By remaining short of the point at which regulation turns into reorganization, the first model fails to create any mechanism for reinvention of the market order in the service of wider participation in the development of knowledge-intensive, experimental production.

The second model—unitary trade and industrial policy—restricts the institutional reshaping of the market economy to the empowerment of a supposedly all-seeing state. Such a state prefers some businesses or sectors to others as the anointed carriers of economic progress. It is activist with regard to sectors, presuming to discern which sectors are "carriers of the future." But it is passive with respect to institutions, except that it requires a state powerful enough to make choices among sectors, playing favorites on the pretense of possessing higher insight.

The epistemological assumptions of my argument for inclusive vanguardism suggest that both these models are misguided. To promote the most advanced practice, we need to innovate in our economic institutions, not just to regulate them more or less aggressively. We should, however, be agnostic about sectors and lines of production even as we are bold in the development of methods and procedures. After all, we know that even in its present insular form the knowledge economy is already multisectoral; it has no exclusive association with any part of the production system. The imposition of unitary trade and industrial policy combines dogmatism about sectors with passive acceptance of the established market order. If the champions of this approach reshape the state they do so only to allow a political and bureaucratic cadre to help some businesses while denying help to others.

The alternative to these two models is a practice of strategic coordination between governments and firms that is decentralized, pluralistic, participatory, and experimental.

Its proximate goal is the same as that of what I described as the first stage of institutional innovation: broadening and orchestrating access to capital and advanced technologies and capabilities. Its ulterior aim is convergence of the rearguards of the national economy to its vanguards in the age of the knowledge economy. Its primary agent is an array of entities established by government and independent from it that pursue different approaches in the same or different parts of the economy, the better to diversify the material available for competitive selection by the market.

Think of such entities as analogous to the agricultural extension programs that evolved in an earlier historical period. They may need to be publicly funded only at the outset: they may subsequently be financed by fees for their services or by equity stakes in the businesses that they lift up or by some combination of equity and debt, and the managers and staffs may share in the gains and risks of this activity. The method of their work is one of decentralized, comparative experimentation with the steps by which rearguards turn into vanguards in each part of the economy.

On the horizontal axis of relations among firms, the changed legal and institutional framework of the market would allow and encourage cooperative competition among small and medium-sized companies: businesses that by virtue of their scale present no risk of suppressing competition. Such firms could pool certain resources while continuing to compete against one another, the better to achieve scale and to build together an apparatus of production with the attributes of the deepened and widespread knowledge economy.

The most successful regional examples of the insular knowledge economy in the United States and Western Europe are characterized by a circulation of people, practices, and ideas among firms, subject only (and not always) to the limits imposed by corporate, employment, and property law. We might view this circulation as the first moment of cooperative competition. The second moment is reliance on ongoing, incompletely bargained relational contracts among firms to organize certain lines of production: for example, among biotechnology or pharmaceutical firms in the United States. The third moment is the development, beyond relational contract, of the practices and private law of cooperative competition.

Contemporary innovations in the relations between governments and firms as well as in the relations among firms already exemplify the principle that the market economy is not there on a take-it-or-leave-it basis. We are not limited to regulating it or to attenuating its inequalities through recourse to corrective redistribution. We can reshape it and by reshaping it influence the primary distribution of economic advantage.

Such changes in the legal and institutional architecture of the knowledge economy look back to the broadening of access to crucial resources and opportunities in favor of a wider range of incumbent or new firms. They look forward to more radical novelty and diversity in the terms on which individuals and firms can enlist capital (broadly defined) in the service of production.

A third stage of innovations in the legal and institutional structure of the market order would begin with change in the property regime, which defines the terms for the decentralization of economic initiative and the claims of economic agents on the means of production. The point would not be to replace the unified property right, established and theorized only in the nineteenth century, by another, equally exclusive form of property vested, for example, in the firm's labor force. The aim instead would be to radically diversify the forms of decentralized access to capital and the other means of production.

The traditional unified property right joins all the powers that we associate with property (and that the civil law tradition distinguished as use, usufruct—command of the income stream, and dominion—the right to alienate or sell) and vests them in a single right holder, the owner. Unified property would become only one of several property regimes, coexisting experimentally alongside other regimes in the same market order. As a result, the market economy would cease to be fastened to a single version of itself. The freedom to recombine factors of production within an unchanged framework of production and exchange would develop into a larger power to innovate in the legally defined institutional arrangements of the market. The result would be to strengthen, rather than to suppress or replace, the logic of economic decentralization: its preference for experiment by many hands over the claim of omniscience by central power.

An advantage of the unified property right is that it allows a risk-taking entrepreneur to do something in which no one else believes without having to avoid potential vetoes by multiple stakeholders. Its disadvantage is the reverse side of this benefit. It fails to provide a legal setting for the superimposition of stakes of different kinds, held by multiple stakeholders, in the same productive resources. For that use, we need fragmentary, conditional, or temporary property rights, resulting from the disaggregation of unified property.

The method of such disaggregation is well established. It was the normal condition of property, even in the West, before the nineteenth century. Moreover, it exists as well in the economies and law of the present day. For example, financial derivatives, including the basic list of options, puts, and calls, are exactly what their name suggests: products designed to create markets in fragmentary elements of the otherwise unified property right. The understanding and application of the principle of disaggregation remain dramatically narrowed, as the unified property right continues to be taken as the standard form of property, although surrounded by a thickening penumbra of deviations from the model that it embodies.

Because it facilitates contrarian entrepreneurial initiative, the unified property right will continue to be useful and even indispensable to the development of the knowledge economy. But rather than remaining the default way to decentralize economic initiative, it would turn over time into a limiting case. The more common form of the property right would become its disaggregation into fragmentary, temporary, or conditional claims on the means of production.

Such disaggregation would organize the coexistence of claims by different stakeholders—such as private or public investors, workers, local governments, and local communities—in the same productive resources. It would make it possible to increase the decentralization of economic initiative—the number of economic agents able to bargain on their own initiative and their own account. It would do so, however, by compromising the nearly absolute and enduring control that the unified property right grants to the right holder, the owner, within the perimeter of the zone of entitlement that it marks out. It was because of this all-inclusive quality that nineteenth-century legal thought took property to be the paradigm of right.

The development of the law and theory of disaggregated property reveals a hidden contradiction in the traditional, unified conception of the property right. That conception supposes that the two most abstract dimensions of the right for organizing decentralization of economic initiative—the amount of economic decentralization (the multiplication of economic agents entitled to bargain on their own initiative and their own account) and the unconditional and almost unlimited control that each of these agents enjoys over the resources at his command—go naturally and necessarily together. In fact, these two sides of property are not only distinct, they are also in tension with each other. We may hope to increase the range and variety of economic agents by cutting back on the uniform, absolute, and perpetual character of the control that each agent exercises. Failure to recognize this tension in the abstract idea of property has been one of the most important reasons for the persistence of the idea that unified property is somehow the central and exemplary feature of a market economy.

An area of reform in the property regime that is vital to the future of the knowledge economy is intellectual property. The established law of patent and copyright—largely a creation of the nineteenth century, inhibits the development of an inclusive vanguardism. It does so chiefly by imposing a highly restrictive grid on the ways in which economic agents can participate in the development of the knowledge economy and share in its rewards. Its practical effect is to help a small number of mega-enterprises dominate the vanguards of production by holding exclusive rights to key technologies that they have either developed themselves or bought from the original inventors. The excuse for concentrating such rents in a small set of capital-rich economic agents is the need to provide incentives to innovation, compensating those who have made long bets on an improbable future. The consequence, however, is to benefit a few only by discouraging and excluding many. It also further enhances the already overwhelming advantages of large scale in the control of the knowledge economy.

A special problem and a unique opportunity exist with respect to the part of the knowledge economy that trades in the data of millions of people. There a change in the law of intellectual property would have the most immediate and revolutionary effect. By contrast, the present arrangements, allowing platform companies to monetize personal data without compensation to the individuals whose activities the data track, aggravate the perversity of the established regime of intellectual property. That regime awards a handful of giant firms exclusive rights to crucial innovations through patent, copyright, trademark, and other rights in intellectual property while leaving empty-handed the millions of creators of the material on which the business model of the platform companies depends.

I outline a program for the transformation of intellectual property here in my description of the third stage of the legal-institutional changes that might serve an inclusive knowledge economy. Much, however, in the proposed changes could and should be anticipated in the earlier moments of this reconstruction of the market order. Two series of reforms of intellectual property have paramount importance. The first group of reforms regards the control of personal data and of claims to their economic value by the individuals whose lives and tastes the data concern. The second set of reforms has to do with the demotion of the patent and copyright laws in their present form to one of several ways of compensating innovators and organizing the use of their discoveries and inventions.

Data should belong to the individuals who generate them, as part of the expression of personality in society. Those who use data for economic gain should win consent for their use and pay for them. The radical decentralization of property in data—a vital input of much of the knowledge economy—would encourage a wide range of varieties of compensation other than the payment of a rent by the data user to the data generator. Such alternative variants of remuneration would include fractional equity stakes. The stakes can in turn be pooled in a secondary market that would monetize and trade them.

Such diversity in the mechanisms of consent and compensation might in turn lead to a more fertile plurality of degrees of engagement of the data creators in the business of the data users. The deepening and detailing of individual data profiles might sometimes have as their counterpart participation of the data creator in some aspect of the business, remunerated by money payments or by equity. The result would be to turn otherwise passive sources of material into engaged agents.

Copyright, patent, and their counterparts in present law should lose their preeminent and nearly exclusive status as mainstays of intellectual property. We should recast them as parts of a wider range of ways of organizing, encouraging, and protecting innovative activity in production. Such activity lies at the center of the knowledge economy. The new advanced practice promises to relax and even reverse what has been up till now the unyielding constraint of diminishing marginal returns to increasing inputs in production. The prospect of keeping this promise rests on the perpetual rather than episodic character of innovation. The innovations characteristic of the knowledge economy take place, without interruption, from within the production system itself, not only through the application of science pursued outside that system.

Imagine then a spectrum of approaches to intellectual property, arranged along a continuum from exclusive ownership to a commons of open access. At one pole of this spectrum would be copyright, patent, and the other rights composing the stock-in-trade of today's intellectual property regime. These rights are modeled on the unified property right of the nineteenth century, with its characteristic focus on the bright line between what is owned by a single personal or corporate owner and what is open to all. It is an arrangement that may continue to be useful or even necessary when, as in the pharmaceutical and biotechnology industries, innovation requires the commitment of a large amount of private capital, over a long time and with great risk. To the extent, however, that the state contributes to the innovation, it should exact in return either a stake in the product of the effort (e.g., special-purpose public–private joint ventures) or some restraint on the power of the owner to restrict free access to his intellectual property.

Instead of abolishing the present regime of intellectual property, we should cut it down to size by turning it into only one of several ways to protect and organize innovation, not the only way. It would apply to some situations but not to many others. The basic justification for keeping it, albeit in a diminished role, is the same as the case for the traditional unified property right itself. Unified, nearly absolute property allows an entrepreneur to run risks and take initiatives that no one else will accept and to be rewarded for his boldness if he succeeds. Just as the unified property right should be only one among many ways of organizing decentralized access to productive resources and opportunities, so the exclusive, income-generating prerogatives granted by patent and copyright should be only one of many arrangements for the encouragement of innovation and the safeguarding of its achievements.

At the other pole of the spectrum would be the placement of an innovation in the public domain, with or without rewards and returns to the innovators given in exchange for denying them the exclusive ownership of their inventions.

In between these two poles of the spectrum, from exclusive property to open access, the knowledge economy should be able to count on a series of alternative arrangements to incentivize innovations and distribute claims to the income streams that they generate. Each would be suited to a distinct range of circumstances likely to arise in a knowledge economy as it spreads and deepens. Here are three such alternatives, set out on a scale of mounting complexity and of growing distance from the law of intellectual property now in force, with modest variations, in all the richest economies.

A first and simplest alternative—the one that requires least legal change—is the licensing of free use by those who enjoy the privileges of copyright, patent, trademark, and their extensions. Such is the example of the Creative Commons license first tried out at the beginning of the twenty-first century. It has the advantage of flexibility: for example, it allows the licensor to privilege noncommercial use. However, it suffers from the crucial disadvantage of depending on the unilateral initiative and generosity of a party enjoying the exclusive rights granted by the present system. It is best adapted to benefit not-for-profit activities that seek to use innovations initially designed for commercial purpose.

A second alternative is the development of a practice that was common in the late nineteenth century when the regime of intellectual property began to take its present form. The state organizes prizes for invention and innovation. Such rewards can be one-time transfers of money. They can also be given over time as a percentage of the tax revenues generated by the productive use of the new technology or practice. It is a way of encouraging innovative activity that imposes no restraint on the use of what the innovator has created. It best suits a circumstance that may be unusual in the present but was common in the past and may become common again in the future: the situation of the relatively isolated inventor or inventors working in a noncommercial setting early in the development of a technology and of the ideas to which it gives tangible form. We can assign the conferral of such rewards to public but not governmental entities established by law and financed by government but independent of governmental control. Such bodies would be staffed by leading specialists in different fields.

A third alternative addresses a situation that is even more likely to recur in a developed and inclusive knowledge economy. Many have collaborated in the making of an innovation and in its development for commercial use. They may be individuals, research institutions, or business organizations. The present regime conforms to a rule of winner-take-all: it accords intellectual property to a single owner and gives him the power to exclude all from access to the protected invention and to charge whatever he may be able to extract for its use.

The knowledge economy, however, thrives on cooperative competition and on a circulation of resources, practices, ideas, and people. Some of its achievements will be the product of many hands. An independent public trust or foundation, or a series of them, free from direction by the central government, should be empowered, under rules and standards established in law, to organize special-purpose entities in which the many contributors to the novelty would hold proportionate stakes. The degree and duration of the right that stakeholders would enjoy to exclude others from free access to their innovation and to charge for its use would be a matter of judgment in the design of each such special-purpose entity. The relative sizes of their stakes would depend on their respective contributions. The criteria for circumscribing all their stakes would include the relative novelty of the invention and the extent to which it resulted from their insight and initiative rather than from the general level of scientific, technological, and technical advance in a particular area of production. An administrative and arbitral case law refining such standards would soon develop. The law would not need to choose between absolute ownership and open access or among multiple claimants to recognition in the collective authorship of an innovation.

The second and third alternatives in this middle space between all and nothing in intellectual property have as one of their premises an advance in institutional design: the establishment of public, not governmental, entities. Among such entities are the trusts or public foundations that would distribute prizes for innovation or recognize the co-authorship of a technological breakthrough by establishing special-purpose funds to hold the proportionate stakes of the innovators and exact a stipulated return for the use of their joint creations. Among them are also—to recall an earlier moment in this argument about the legal-institutional architecture of the knowledge economy—the boards representing civil society in the governance of platform companies that we hesitate to break up for fear of losing the social and economic value resulting from the size of their communities of users.

An inclusive knowledge economy is the child of a society and of a culture with the attributes that I have explored in earlier parts of this book. We should not treat it as the creature of either the market or the state alone. Society beyond the state and the market should be represented in the governance and organization of a knowledge economy that it has helped create. Nowhere is there greater reason for such representation than in the establishment and assignment of claims to share in the gains of innovation and invention. The need to reform intellectual property stands as an instance of a general argument: a widespread and deepened form of knowledge-intensive production requires the institutional and legal remaking of the market economy.

That the deepening and diffusion of the knowledge economy must rely on renewal in the vocabulary of private law and property, including intellectual property, is already shown by what I described as an earlier stage in the evolution of its legal architecture: decentralized strategic coordination between governments and firms and cooperative competition among firms. Those institutional developments point in the direction of arrangements that encourage and organize the combination of private and governmental initiative and give legal shape to the coexistence of multiple stakes, held by many different kinds of stakeholders, in the same productive resources.

It is only a beginning. Achievement of the potential of the market economy through its simultaneous radicalization and diffusion requires us to lift the restraints continuing to weigh on our experiments with the institutional and legal form of economic decentralization. The forms that are good for some purposes are inadequate for others.

The epistemological case for a market economy is the superiority of experimental diversity to dogmatic uniformity as a route to discovering what we can achieve in the economy as well as how we can achieve it. If the market order is to be the institutional expression of experimentalism, the experimentalist impulse must apply as well to that expression: we must not allow the market order to be fastened to a single, exclusive version of itself. We must turn its institutional and legal reinvention into part of its everyday business. We must refuse to put the constitutive arrangements of the market beyond the reach of its defining impulse to establish an ordered and creative anarchy.

14.

Background Incitements: Generalized Experimentalism and High-Energy Democracy

What background conditions make it more likely that we will be able to satisfy the requirements of the widespread and developed form of the knowledge economy, which the previous three sections have explored? These background conditions are of two kinds: those that have to do with culture and consciousness and those that relate to the reshaping of democracy.

We should not treat these features of culture and politics as antecedent conditions that need to be fulfilled before we can have any hope of pressing forward an agenda of inclusive vanguardism. To view them in that way would be to commit the mistake of seeing this program as a system that we must implement either altogether or not at all. We may be able to progress on any of the foreground requirements before we hit against the constraints imposed by failure to satisfy the background conditions. Progress in changing the foreground may itself begin to change the cultural and political background: foreground and background are reciprocally connected in a process of combined and uneven development.

Moreover, the accomplishment of the background conditions has value far transcending its usefulness to the cause of an inclusive knowledge economy. At stake is the raising of our powers and of our experience to a higher level. The development and spread of the knowledge economy would be only part of this larger transformation.

The background condition in culture to the deepening and dissemination of the knowledge economy is the generalization of an experimentalist impulse in every part of social life. The presence of that impulse in the economy enhances it everywhere else in society. Its noneconomic expressions in turn reinforce its economic presence.

Consider some of the incitements to the generalization of the experimentalist impulse beyond the economy as well as within it. One is an education that adopts a dialectical approach to received knowledge. The habit of distinguishing dominant ideas from the way things are, inspired by presenting all knowledge from opposing points of view, protects against reliance on established opinion and invites lifelong questioning.

Another stimulus is the provision of opportunities and supports for midlife change of careers. Such help must be both educational and financial. It would encourage the reinvention of the self that the neo-romantic culture of the freest and richest contemporary societies promotes but rarely supports.

By far the most important incitement to the generalization of an experimentalist impulse is the provision of a social inheritance: a package of economic endowments and safeguards settled on all individuals, according to a country's level of wealth. This social inheritance—inheritance by everyone of something from the state rather than of much by a few from their moneyed families—makes it possible to remain fearless in the midst of surrounding change, uncertainty, and conflict. The relative entrenchment of a set of endowments and protections safeguarding against the ups and downs of the economy and of politics serves as the indispensable counterpart to the throwing open of everything else in society to challenge and change. Its ideal goal is to turn everyone into the Seraph Abdiel in *Paradise Lost*: unmoved, unshaken, unseduced, unterrified.

Consider the core meaning of the experimentalist impulse both as a way of acting and as a way of understanding.

As a way of acting, it diminishes the distance between the ordinary moves that we make within an unchanged and unchallenged framework and the extraordinary moves by which we challenge and change pieces of that framework. It turns the latter into a habitual prolongation of the former. Institutional changes like those that I propose here in the organization of the economy and of politics draw our context-preserving and our context-changing activities lastingly together. The work of the experimentalist impulse is to foreshadow the effect of such institutional change just as political virtue may prefigure institutional reform and institutions may economize on virtue.

As a way of understanding, the experimentalist impulse relaxes our dependence on established methods and presuppositions in each part of knowledge and experience. It prompts us to see on the basis of alternative presuppositions and to grasp one part of experience with methods habitually applied to another.

Schopenhauer remarked that a talented man is a marksman who hits a target that others cannot hit; a genius is a marksman who hits a target that others cannot see. A hope of the democrat and of the experimentalist is that larger vision, which forms part of a higher life for the ordinary man and woman, need not depend on genius; it can become a common possession. To become a common possession, it must exist as the fragmentary and largely unspoken epiphanies of an ordinary life rather than as an explicit and comprehensive message conveyed by the prophet-genius to his contemporaries. Viewed in this light, the generalization of the experimentalist impulse represents yet another instance of the enlargement of the ordinary, which it is the higher purpose of an inclusive vanguardism to promote.

The other background condition favoring our ability to satisfy the foreground requirements of an inclusive vanguardism has to do with the organization of democratic politics: the development of a high-energy democracy that dispenses with crisis as the circumstance enabling radical reform, overthrows the rule of the living by the dead, and makes every part of the structure of the economy susceptible in fact—not just in theory—to radical reform expressed in law. As it continues to exist in an unequal society, such a democracy must be so designed that its institutions can resist capture by the most powerful and organized interests.

A collective dictatorship exercised by a political and technocratic elite claiming to rule in the national interest and condemning its population to an obsequious political silence offers a costly shortcut to these aims. It deprives the country of the chance to combine open debate with organized experimentation in the definition and development of a path. It therefore makes the future of society hostage to the dogmatic preconceptions of the ruling elite. It allows every wider proposal for policy or institutional change to be judged by the test of its relation to the power interest of the collective dictatorship. It creates a social world forever at risk of seeing political power translated into economic advantage and economic advantage into political influence. It avoids being undermined by favoritism and corruption only by delivering itself to a yet more vigilant and meddlesome despotism. And it prompts the collective despots to seek in their association with an inherited orthodoxy a basis of legitimacy more powerful and enduring than the vagaries of prosperity. As the words of that orthodoxy lose their meaning over time, the dictators find themselves forced to invent other meanings for them, calculated to combine adaptation to changing circumstance with their stake in the preservation of rule.

China has provided the most important instance of such a political life. Its wealth of micro-institutional experiments in ways of associating firms with governments and local communities or with one another might have served as a point of departure for the reshaping of the economy in the direction I have described. Instead, these novel forms of economic decentralization have remained largely confined to the role of reconciling state capitalism and collective dictatorship with the familiar worldwide understanding of what a market economy can and should look like.

All the democracies that exist in the world, however, are weak democracies. They allow for only a pale political rendition of the contending forces in society. Their arrangements permit enough contrast of orientation among parts of the state to result in impasse, and then perpetuate the impasse rather than resolving it quickly and decisively. They treat strong central initiative and devolution of authority to local government as if they were inversely related when in fact we can and should hope to have more of both. With rare exceptions, they keep the citizenry at a low level of engagement in political life—sleeping when ruin and war do not awaken them—and fail to enrich representative democracy with elements of direct or participatory democracy. As a result, they are easily captured by organized interests. They inhibit the practice of radical reform except when an economic crisis or a military conflict serves as the enabling circumstance of such change.

Weak democracy is the product of three factors. The first is an inadequate idea of democratic politics. The second is an unacceptably restricted repertoire of institutional forms—including constitutional arrangements—on which the design of a democratic state can draw. The third is failure to appreciate the contradiction between the promise and premises of democratic politics and the realities of existence in a society that continues to assign people starkly unequal life chances. It is the paradoxical ambition of democracy to give voice to people's understanding of their interests, ideals, and identities without allowing political life simply to echo and reinforce social and economic inequality: an ambition summarized in the abstract conception of equal rights and equal citizenship.

A strong democracy able to master the inherited structure of social life and to subject it to perennial testing cannot be understood as simply the self-government of the majority qualified by the right of political minorities to become a future majority and cultivate dissent and divergence in the meantime. The idea of democracy must include the perpetual creation of the new and the transcendence and triumph of society over its received arrangements.

The institutional history of democracy presents us with an unacceptable choice. On one side is a highly restricted and restrictive set of alternative constitutional arrangements tried out in the course of modern Western history and exported from there to the rest of the world. These arrangements bear the marks, and help produce the consequences, of weak democracy. On the other side is the dream of a direct democracy of councils or "soviets," aroused in moments of insurrectionary fervor only to give way, when they fail as they always have, to despotism or weak democracy. The revolutionary interlude in routine political life, like the romantic interruption of the routines of married life, disturbs established structure momentarily without affording any prospect of a lasting change in the relation of settled arrangements to our structure-defying freedom.

A high-energy democracy must not serve as the passive reflection and reinforcement of the inequalities of a class society. To give practical substance to political equality, its institutions must be designed to neutralize the political influence of class advantage. It is not enough that by affirming the prerogatives of equal citizenship they embody a way of connecting people that is in tension with the realities of a hierarchically segmented economy. In such an economy most people remain condemned to economically dependent wage labor or to involuntary self-employment as a disguised form of economic dependence. Democratic institutions must provide a setting for the innovations that over time disrupt and transform the features of economic life that put experiences of servitude and belittlement in the place of what democracy promises to everyone: a chance to share in shaping the collective context of individual initiative.

To this end, the doctrine and practice of democracy need to expand to include the establishment of political arrangements that not only facilitate their own revision but that also deprive the economic order—the institutional and legal constitution of the market economy—of any claim to lie beyond the reach of political reinvention and remaking. The expansion of our view of democracy in this direction would be meaningless if it failed to have as its counterpart the enlargement of the narrow stock of ways of organizing democratic politics and a democratic state that are now on offer in the world.

The institutional forms useful to the achievement of such a democracy depend on the circumstances and history of each country. Outside the speculations of philosophers, institutional innovation never works on a blank slate. It can move in a direction with radically transformative implications like the one I have just sketched. It nevertheless takes as its point of departure the ideas, institutions, and practices available in its historical moment and in its national circumstances. It advances most often by enlarging, through analogical extension and recombination, the established institutional options in the country and in the world.

Its institutional handiwork should not be subservient to a sectarian and transient agenda in political economy; it should be able to accommodate and to organize in the political life of the people the contest and succession of such agendas. It cannot, however, hope to remain neutral in the clash of visions of the good. In aspiring to the realistic goal of openness to diversity of experience, of interest, and of aspiration and in multiplying occasions for its own remaking, it should renounce the false and dangerous claim of neutrality, invariably invoked in support of its opposite: the effort to entrench, together with the political regime, an economic and social fix on an established form of social and economic life.

High-energy democracy is the most useful political background to a deepened and widespread knowledge economy. But it cannot be imagined, justified, or developed solely on the basis of that change in our economic life. Its motivations and attractions lie in the interests and ideals served by the inclusive vanguardism that I have described and in our overriding stake in the creation of a structure that eases and organizes its own improvement.

This democratic ideal expresses our view of ourselves as agents who contain more than the social and conceptual worlds that they build and inhabit. It is this larger view of agency, empowerment, and transcendence that is manifest in the conception of a high-energy democracy. It might take many other economic forms, at odds with the program of economic reconstruction that I have outlined here.

Four nontrivial principles of institutional design mark out the path of movement toward the institutions of a high-energy democracy responsive to the standards discussed in the preceding pages. We must craft such institutions in detail in the light of circumstance and history and with the institutional materials and ideas at hand as well as with those that we can add to them. We should not be discouraged: if there is clarity about the direction, the modesty of our initial steps and their subjection to circumstantial constraint will not prevent us and our successors from achieving far-reaching change. These principles are general and abstract. They are not, however, empty: they cannot be reconciled with most of the constitutional arrangements and political institutions and practices of the weak democracies of today.

The first is *the principle of the political expression, arousal, and empowerment of group difference.* This principle commands us to organize democratic politics so that it not only reflects a wide range of conflict of interests and of visions in society but also provides these clashing tendencies with the means to sharpen and develop their differences. In the economy the fecundity of a method of competitive, market-based selection depends on the richness of the material from which competitive selection selects. So, too, the experimentalist culture of a high-energy democracy finds inspiration in a great wealth of contending interests and identities.

These clashing perspectives need to win a political voice: hence the preference in most (but not all) circumstances for proportional representation and multiple rounds of balloting rather than first-past-the-post electoral regimes and conclusive decision on a single ballot. For the same reason, the state must have many parts, so that a tendency of interest or opinion that fails to find expression in one

part may secure it in another. The danger that the manifes-
tation of conflict not only in politics but in the state will
lead to paralysis of coherent initiative is addressed by the
second principle, of rapid resolution of impasse.

It is not enough for politics and the state to reflect manifest differences in society. A high-energy democracy brings
these differences out and arouses them rather than
suppressing them. When one such view gains control of
part of the state or part of the country, it helps difference
turn into tangible initiative. Thus, the third principle will
say that as society goes down a certain path, it should
hedge its bets and allow parts of the country or of the
economy to diverge from dominant law and policy and
present to the country the image of another path. Its public
culture should not outlaw, in the name of civic harmony,
the political expression of religious belief or discourage
the religious criticism of one religion, or worldview, by
another. Its aim will not be to provide a cool public space,
sealed off from the sources of most passionate disagree-
ment. It will be to expand that space of the political and to
break down the barriers separating it from the full, contra-
dictory life of society and culture.

The deliberate arousal of conflictual diversity, not just its
passive representation in politics, may seem to place society at the brink of perpetual disunion. It may appear to do
so in exchange for no clear benefit other than the dubious
advantage of investing politics with the hopes and fears
nourished in other departments of our experience. In fact,
the clash of interests and visions need bring disunion only
if it is simplified: if all the differences of interest and opinion are made to align and the citizenry is broken up into a

few tribes, each defined by the marriage of a wide range of interests with a characteristic set of opinions. If, however, people are divided along many cross-cutting lines there will be no such simplification. Difference will proliferate and intensify without reducing political society to the condition of two or three warring camps.

Liberal political theory has sometimes supposed this multiplication of non-coterminous difference to be the natural condition of a complex and pluralistic society living under democracy. In fact, the degree to which this supposedly natural condition prevails may depend on the organization of politics: on whether it suppresses difference, or simplifies it, or prompts it to flourish, not least by seeking in political action the means to develop it.

Moreover, the will to collective difference, by the nation-state and its agents or by groups within the nation-state, is dangerous to the extent that it is reduced to a will to be different deprived of the power to create actual difference. The will to difference, without the power to create actual difference, turns into group hatred. A group or a people hates another, close by, not because it is different but because it wants to be different and is becoming alike. The solution is not to suppress the pursuit of difference; it is to equip it. A willed difference can only be the cause and object of an unyielding and frustrated faith. Actual difference is porous, impure, and ambiguous, and invites syncretism and compromise in practice even where there is zealotry and intransigence in doctrine.

We can nevertheless ask what good this principle of the arousal of difference serves, other than incitement to a widening of the range of collective experiment. The answer is: vitality and strength—of individuals and of forms of social life—forged in the midst of contrast and conflict: each nation, each distinctive set of affinities and associations within the nation, and each individual represents an experiment in humanity. Given that society has no natural and necessary form, we can develop our powers only by developing them in different directions. Diversity is the means, not the end. The end is to come more fully into the possession of life, to become the original that one is—as a state organized to shield a distinctive form of life and as an individual who is formed both by and against the multiple groups to which he belongs.

The enemy of the principle of the recognition, arousal, and empowerment of difference is a crude opposition, in the organization of economic and political life, between order and anarchy. According to this prejudice, any break in order represents the beginning of a slide into anarchy. All the higher forms of economic and political order are characterized by the encouragement of a dialectic of contrasting experiences and ideas the better to inspire and inform self-correction. The deeper and widespread form of the knowledge economy exemplifies in its own domain of production this splitting of the difference between order and anarchy, and so must its basis in economic and political institutions. The ideal limit of this conception is the notion of an ordered anarchy that acknowledges and sustains the surfeit of life over structure.

The remaining three institutional principles of a high-energy democracy can be stated more briefly. They qualify both one another and the first principle.

The second principle is the *principle of the rapid and decisive resolution of impasse*. The arousal and empowerment of difference in society and its expression in politics and in the organization of the state create the risk of paralysis: the opposing forces, interests, and visions may reduce one another to relative impotence.

Each part of social and economic life must be organized to favor the breaking of such paralysis through decisive action rather than through half-hearted compromise. To perpetuate deadlock is to deprive ourselves of the benefit of developing and trying out clearly delineated alternatives. It is to risk a succession of second-best solutions in each area of our collective activity.

If impasse cannot be overcome in a particular domain of social life, its resolution falls to politics, which sets, through law, the ultimate terms of the transformation of every domain of social and economic practice. The state is itself susceptible to being paralyzed by impasse if it contains—as the first principle suggests that it should—a multiplicity of parts or branches that can suffer the influence of different combinations of interest and opinion and serve as independent sources of initiative. The import of the second principle is not to avoid these instances of paralyzing contradiction within the state; it is to break deadlock quickly and make strong central initiative possible.

The constitutional implications of this view are best illustrated by identifying the constitutional plans that it excludes. On the one side, it stands opposed to a plan like Madison's scheme of checks and balances that perpetuates impasse in divided government, and treats such perpetuation as a solution rather than as a problem because it inhibits the use of politics to reshape the economy and the society. On the other hand, it also rejects a pure parliamentary system like the one into which the British political regime has evolved because it favors a near dictatorship of the head of government. Its impulse is to suppress conflict within the government and the state and to diminish the extent to which contradiction of interest and of vision within society is reflected in government. The point is not to ensure strong central initiative by suppressing or avoiding conflict, even conflict within the state itself. It is to excite conflict, in the state as well as within society, but then to resolve it. The conflict then takes new form, hastening the pace of politics.

The constitutional plan of the United States is based on a deliberate confusion of the liberal principle of the fragmentation of power—within the federal government as well as within the federal system—with the conservative principle of the slowing down of politics. An implication of the second principle is to prefer constitutional arrangements that affirm the liberal principle but repudiate the conservative one. The unwritten constitution of the British political regime supposes that the practical advantages of decisive central initiative can be achieved only by containing or forestalling in the first place the expression of conflict in the state. The cost is then to forego the benefits justifying the first principle and to achieve unity of governmental action only by renouncing the advantages of regulated disunion.

These remarks may suggest a preference for semi-presidential regimes of the kind that became common in

European constitutions, especially in the decades after the Second World War. However, the constitutional architecture of these regimes offers at best a point of departure for enacting these first two principles of institutional design. They do too little to arouse and institutionalize conflict within society and the state, and then, once conflict is established, too little to resolve the conflict rapidly and decisively. For example, the constitution of the French Fifth Republic allows for a slow pace of politics when there is divergence between the president and the parliamentary majority ("cohabitation") rather than working toward a fast pace by facilitating early elections of both president and parliament or appealing to comprehensive programmatic plebiscites and referendums.

The enemy of the second principle is the false assumption of an inverse relation between contradiction in society and its expression in the state, on one side, and the facility for decisive central initiative, on the other side. There can be no strength in a desert of opposing interests and opinions. The aim is to raise the temperature while accelerating the pace: "to make mistakes as quickly as possible."

The third principle in the institutional design of a high-energy democracy is the *principle of devolution*. Strong central initiative, ensured by the rapid resolution of impasse (the second principle) and informed by the arousal and empowerment of difference in society and in the state (the first principle) should be combined with opportunities for part of the country (viewed territorially) or even for part of the economy (viewed sector by sector) to secede from the predominant national path, decided by strong central initiative, and to create countermodels of the national future.

The core intuitive idea motivating this third principle is that as the country proceeds down a certain path it can and should hedge its bets. It should make it possible for defeated or imagined alternatives to be explored in parts of itself. For the exploration to be instructive and persuasive, the countermodel must be tried out in practice; it cannot remain unrealized doctrine. The arousal and empowerment of difference in society and in the state guarantee that there will be no lack of motivations to diverge.

The most straightforward setting in which to apply the principle of devolution is the organization of relations between central and local government, especially in a federal system. Under certain conditions a state or a municipal government might be allowed to depart very far from established federal law and national policy—far more than conventional federalism traditionally allows. A developed countermodel—the organization of part of social and economic life on deviant lines—is likely to involve combined innovation in many connected institutional arrangements and in the parts of law that give them shape.

A premise of conventional federalism is that every part of the federal system—the states relative to one another, and each municipal government in comparison to other municipal governments—must enjoy the same degree of autonomy. The insistence on uniformity in the delegation of authority to make law limits the extent of autonomy, inhibiting more radical deviations.

A state or municipal government should be able to apply to the national legislature and to the courts for the privilege of enacting such a super-deviation. The legislature will decide whether the proposed experiment threatens a national interest. The courts will decide whether it meets two basic standards: that it not be irreversible and that it not have the effect of condemning any group to a form of entrenched disadvantage: disadvantage from which the group cannot readily escape by the forms of economic initiative and political action available to it.

What goes for federal systems holds as well for unitary states, such as France or the United Kingdom. It is sheer doctrinal prejudice that strong central initiative cannot be reconciled in a unitary state with radical devolution. The combination may be even easier to implement and more fertile in its benefits than under a federal system. Such a state will not need to contend with the presumption, characteristic of federalism, that the measure of autonomy must be uniform within the federation. The unitary character of the state creates, at the same time, a political structure that may be naturally hospitable to strong central initiative unless the constitutional arrangements conspire both to divide government and to perpetuate impasse.

Under a federal system and a unitary state alike, there are two ways to reconcile strong central initiative with radical devolution. The first way is for the central initiative to have a comprehensive scope but for only limited parts of the country to exercise the prerogative of wide deviation from the national path. The disposition to exercise this prerogative, with its attendant risks and costs, is likely to prove exceptional. The second way is for both central initiative and radical devolution to be less than comprehensive, advancing in certain parts of social and economic life, but not in others, so that they need not collide—an outcome that is probable, given the selective character of even the most ambitious reform programs.

The enemy of the principle of devolution is the premise that central and devolved power are inversely related: the more power the center has, the less power the periphery— the states and municipal governments—enjoy. This hydraulic model, or this lump-sum view of power, may seem self-evidently true. It is in fact false, as the preceding discussion has illustrated. It results from a failure of institutional imagination.

The fourth principle of the institutional design of high-energy democracy is the *principle of engagement.* It recommends a heightening of the level of organized popular engagement in political life. If the second principle, of the rapid and decisive resolution of impasse, requires a quickening of the pace of politics, this fourth principle supports a raising of the temperature of politics—the degree of organized and therefore sustained mobilization. This raising of the temperature is the high energy to which the term high-energy democracy refers.

The intuitive motivation of the fourth principle is the view that a politics rich in structural content—in the ability to generate and implement alternatives and to innovate, without the provocation of crisis, in everything including its own organization—must be a politics of high engagement. The engagement must not depend on passing tides of civic enthusiasm and disenchantment. It must be supported by institutional arrangements on the premise that institutions economize on political virtue although they cannot dispense with it.

In the weak democracies of today, the people sleep until national emergency awakens them, confirming the dependence of change on crisis. In the meantime, they delegate the management of their affairs to a cadre of professional politicians. The inevitability of this result seems to be confirmed by the repeated failure, during the brief revolutionary interludes in which it has been tried out, of a government of popular councils. The fantasies of radical republican theory, with their demand that private concerns be sacrificed to all-encompassing and selfless civic commitment, have served to make the political culture of weak democracies seem to offer the most realistic, if not the only, chance of political liberty.

The alternative, however, is not to put the selfless citizen in place of the flesh-and-blood, interest-bearing individual of real life or to revive in large societies the hopeless dream of direct democracy from the bottom up. The alternative is to take initiatives that gradually expand the range of our political powers and concerns, allow structural change or radical reform to arise more easily and constantly from normal politics and ordinary life, and dispense with economic or military trauma as the condition of change.

Three sets of legal and institutional innovations are crucial in this regard. The first set are those that have to do with the relation between money and politics: assuring public resources for the financing of political activity and denying private money—as distinguished from the commitment of time—political influence. The second are those that assure to social movements as well as political parties free access to the established means of mass communication, especially television, as a condition of the revocable licenses under which the media companies do their business. The third and most important set are those that enrich representative democracy with elements of direct democracy, without attempting to substitute the latter for the former: for example, through participation of the organized local community in the management of its affairs and the direction of governmental resources; through the engagement of organized civil society, partnering with government, by means of a range of third-sector or cooperative forms, in the experimental provision of public services (including health and education); and through the expanded use of comprehensive as well as single-issue plebiscites and referendums, provided that each such consultation is preceded by ample debate, staged in the means of communication with the widest reach.

These three sets of initiatives help give practical effect to the principle of engagement, while extending and sharpening the political consequences of the principle of the arousal and empowerment of difference. Their cumulative effect is to raise the level of political mobilization in society. For the heightening of engagement to be sustainable it must be experienced as a broadening rather than a sacrifice of our ordinary concerns. Its meaning is to empower us by diminishing the gap between the ordinary moves that we make within a regime of arrangements and assumptions that we take for granted and the extraordinary moves by which— typically pressed or provoked by crisis—we struggle over the revision of some piece of that regime.

The enemy of the fourth principle is the idea that politics must be either institutional and cold or anti-institutional and hot (as in Caesarism). This idea provides a premise of conservative political science but also of the romantic imagination in politics, which despairs of changing the relation between our institutional structures and our structure-defying freedom. The point of the fourth principle is to work toward a politics that is both hot and institutional. It is in that political setting that programs like the project of inclusive vanguardism have the best chance of advancing.

15.

Inclusive Vanguardism and the Dilemma of Economic Development

Having characterized the knowledge economy in both its confined and shallow and its disseminated and deepened form and explored the requirements for its deepening and dissemination as well as the background conditions for the fulfillment of these requirements, I now turn to three larger perspectives on my theme. The first is the relation of inclusive vanguardism to the options faced today by developing countries. The second is its relation to the politics as well as to the political economy of the richest countries in the world. The third is the significance of my argument about the knowledge economy, in its insular or inclusive form, for the most rudimentary feature of economic life: the reciprocal accommodation or recurrent imbalance between supply and demand. This third perspective in turn offers a basis on which to understand the implications of the argument of this book for some central problems in economic theory. It vindicates the conjecture of Adam Smith and Karl Marx that the study of the most advanced practice of production offers the best way to grasp the deepest and most universal features of economic life.

Developing countries today face an apparent dilemma. The formula central to the development economics of the second half of the twentieth century was to catch up to the richest economies by industrializing, if by industrialization we mean establishing Fordist mass production in its canonical form. This formula has stopped working, for reasons that I soon discuss. The alternative to the formula— ascent to a broad-based, inclusive version of the knowledge economy—seems, however, to be inaccessible. If not even the richest economies, with the strongest institutional capabilities and educational resources, seem to have advanced far in this direction, how could one expect the developing countries, even more deficient in the requirements of inclusive vanguardism, to do so?

The old strategy fails. The new one is too demanding and remote to offer a feasible alternative to the old one. Today all thinking about development must begin by engaging with this dilemma: it has become the most pressing practical challenge to economic development, and it exposes the inadequacy of the development ideas that are now available.

Recall the major message of classical development economics. In the long run, according to this view, economic growth is constrained by the fundamentals: education and institutions. As I earlier remarked, despite the lip service that it paid to the making of "human capital," development economics had little to say about the content, the method, and the institutional setting of education. The reason is simple: industrialization in the style of mass production, the real object of desire in classical development economics, required little by way of education. The chief need was for workers to move as their machines did; too much education could spell only trouble.

As to institutions, the other fundamental, development economics was in general satisfied to recommend a barely adjusted version of economic institutions that it had encountered ready-made in its historical circumstance: a regulated mixed-market economy. What mattered is that investors be secure in their property and in the income stream that it generated and that the state have space for a planning apparatus devoted to long-term development strategy and to its translation into short-term policy.

The main message of classical development economics lay elsewhere. The best way to boost economic growth in the short to medium term was to move workers and resources from less to more productive sectors of the economy: in practice from agriculture to industry, in the mode of standardized mass production. The stereotypical character of the technologies and capabilities required by mass production, and the relative modesty of its educational and institutional presuppositions, meant that a boost in productivity and consequently in growth could be achieved in little time. It could continue to advance until it hit against limits through failure to obtain a corresponding advance with respect to the fundamentals. But such a clash with antecedent constraints, rather than being a threat, might serve as a prompt to overcome those limits and continue the transformation that had been initiated by the transfer of workers and resources to the sector occupied by the most advanced practice of production: Fordist industry. In a world economy in which relatively capital-intensive mass production was associated with the richest societies, industrialization meant ascent in the international division of labor.

Developing countries can no longer rely on this prescription to sustain economic growth and begin to close the gap separating them from the richest economies. Some have long suffered from what has been described as premature deindustrialization. Others have tried to prolong the life of mass production by combining low wages (by international standards) with a specialized and subordinate niche in global value chains, useful to the megafirms of knowledge-intensive production. They have embraced the commoditized side of a business that in its upper reaches, typically in a faraway rich country, exemplifies the familiar insular form of experimentalist, knowledge-intensive production. Only a few (especially China and India and to a lesser degree Russia and Brazil) have established, always in the insular mode, an outpost of the cosmopolitan knowledge economy.

There are multiple and connected reasons why the standard industrializing prescription of development economics has stopped working. First, advanced production, from its exclusive bases throughout the world, is increasingly able to outcompete belated mass production. It can do so directly by finding ways to produce more efficiently, and with enhancements, the products of traditional industry. Under the system that I have called hyper-vanguardism, it can also do so by assigning standardized parts of its lines of production to factories that are usually located in other economies with lower wages and taxes. Such enterprise then becomes a satellite to global lines of production—the sidekick—rather than the vanguard that development economics saw it as being.

Second, in this context, traditional industrialization ceases to be associated with ascent in the international division of labor. The more telling line of division in the global economy is no longer between industry and everything else—especially agriculture. It is between the fringe of advanced production established in every sector, including (scientific) agriculture, and everything else.

Third, the distinctions among sectors, a crucial premise of the message of classical development economics, lose force. The hardness of these distinctions represents a sign of relative backwardness. The knowledge economy in all its forms, shallow and confined, or developed and widespread, subverts them. It especially undermines the difference between manufacturing and services.

Fourth, mass production industry continues to be viable, where it survives, only on the basis of a race to lower wages and to a lower tax take, as labor and tax arbitrage comes to drive the location of backward manufacturing. Cheap labor and the denial to the state of resources for public investment in people and in their capabilities as well as in the transport, communication, and energy infrastructure of production discourage movement toward the vanguard.

But what is the alternative to the broken formula of classical development economics? (The development economics that succeeded it has largely abandoned any general view and prescription. It has sought refuge in microstudies of the differential effects of different policies on the poor. Classical development economics had a defective structural vision. Its successor, in consonance with the predominant line of contemporary social science, prefers to have no structural vision at all.) The alternative would be a shift in the direction of inclusive vanguardism, by means of the intermediate steps that may be needed, in the circumstances of a developing economy today, to get from here to there.

At this point, however, those who search for an alternative to the old message may well feel despondent. If inclusive vanguardism remains a seemingly heroic and improbable project even in those economies that seem least remote from its promises, how can it be implemented in societies in which its educational, moral, and institutional requirements seem even farther from fulfillment? These are on the whole countries that continue to struggle with the basics of education and law and that often veer between extremes of inequality and a churning of directions and regimes that is interrupted only by open or veiled despotism. How, their citizens might object, can you ask us for the maximum when our grasp on the minimum remains weak?

Before considering a response to this objection, think of how the problem presents itself in a particular economy: Brazil of the early twenty-first century. The example will suggest why the challenge presented by the task of pursuing inclusive vanguardism is inescapable for developing as well as for richer economies. It will also help us begin to redefine the problem in ways that render it amenable to solution.

The heart of Brazilian industry set down in the southeast of the country, and especially in the state of São Paulo, under the inspiration of classical development economics, was mass production. Even when first established, it was already belated. It reached, and has ever since generally maintained, standards of excellence in manufacturing. It has done so, however, under the incubus of what has increasingly become a style of industrial production that is retrograde in its technological and organizational core. This belated Fordism remains competitive only at the cost of severe restraints on returns to labor and dependence on state support, often in the form of subsidized credit and of the tax favors handed out under cover of vulgar Keynesianism.

The knowledge economy has made an appearance in Brazil but only in severely insular form: as start-ups and high-tech manufacturing and services in a few places in the country. A remarkable network of quasi-state technical schools and support centers—a legacy of the corporatism of the Vargas years—has supported these isolated initiatives in advanced manufacturing. The state has at its command powerful public banks, including one of the largest development banks in the world. It also has an entity devoted to the most difficult and least common form of assistance to small business: guidance in the enhancement of productive practices—an extension service outside agriculture. The doctrine developed in the practice of that guidance included the concept of "local productive arrangements," describing decentralized partnerships of governments with emergent firms and cooperative competition among such firms.

A figure that plays a strategic role in most contemporary economies—the advanced middle-size firm—is, however, largely missing. And none of the institutional equipment of the Brazilian state or of the doctrines of development— from import-substituting industrialization to the pursuit of financial confidence—has saved the country from becoming one of the most striking examples of premature deindustrialization. In the wake of the commodity-price boom of the first decade of the twenty-first century and of Chinese demand for agricultural, ranching, and mining products, manufacturing has declined dramatically as a percentage of both output and exports. Rather than being replaced or converted, belated Fordism simply shrank. Brazil found itself becoming old before it had become rich, and losing mass production before it had acquired the knowledge economy.

Meanwhile, the country continued to support one of the most vibrant entrepreneurial cultures in the world. That culture found a powerful carrier in a second, mixed-race, petty bourgeoisie and in millions of still poor Brazilian workers who sought to follow the path of this class and embraced its culture of self-help and initiative. They did so without having the means to realize their aspirations.

In some of the poorest parts of the country, like the semi-arid backlands of the Northeast, it was possible to find regions, such as the textile industry of the interior of Pernambuco, in which a range of practices, legal entities, and even technologies of European market economies coexisted, from the putting-out system of the seventeenth century to the old-fashioned mass production of the late twentieth century. This wealth of entrepreneurial spirit remained largely unequipped and directionless, and yet almost miraculously resilient. Here was the raw material for a new agenda of national development, if only such an agenda were on offer.

The question presented by these circumstances was whether the whole country would need first to become the São Paulo of the mid-twentieth century in order later to become something else, pining in the purgatory of belated Fordism, or whether it and its government could organize a direct passage from pre- to post-Fordism outside the old industrial centers of the Southeast. The former answer to this question seemed to offer no hope for all the reasons enumerated at the beginning of this section: to retread the earlier path would not achieve the earlier results. But the latter answer seemed to require an accomplishment for which there existed no ready-made model in the world. It was simply the Brazilian form of the dilemma of development described in the preceding pages.

My Brazilian example illustrates several aspects of this dilemma. The first point is that it is a false dilemma. The advancement of inclusive vanguardism is difficult under any conditions, especially the conditions of a developing country. To respond to this difficulty, however, by trying to give an afterlife to traditional industry is worse than difficult; it is futile. Such industry can no longer serve as the vehicle of "unconditional convergence" that classical development economics took it to be, and has ever less of a chance of working for all the reasons I discussed earlier.

Because industrial mass production has ceased to be the most advanced productive practice, the message of classical development economics assumes a less confident and more qualified tone. It tells the developing country: industrialize conventionally and wait your turn in line. This message has the appeal of apparent modesty; it proposes persistence in a well-known path. It fails, however, to take account of irreversible changes in the evolution of our productive capabilities and consequently as well in the world division of labor.

The argument for it depends on the view that all economies must follow the same relentless evolutionary sequence, rehearsing in a later historical period as their future the past of the economies that have overtaken them. The nature of the most advanced practice of production has not changed in a single place. It has changed, and is manifest, in all the major economies of the world. Its presence undermines, both directly and through its influence on the international division of labor, the uses of mass production as an instrument of ascent to a higher level of national development. In the Brazilian example, an attempt to turn the rest of the Brazilian economy into the São Paulo of the mid-twentieth century would produce something unlike that vanished world: a throwback understood to be both a retreat and a surrender—a retreat from the global vanguard, and a surrender to the countries and businesses that have reached the frontier of production.

The second point illustrated by the Brazilian example is the abundant presence in Brazil, as in much of the world, of the prime ingredient of inclusive vanguardism. It is not one of the conditions (discussed in previous sections) that distinguish it from earlier most advanced practices of production. It is a resource crucial to the making of all such advanced practices: a restless vitality and entrepreneurial impulse widely distributed in society. Its characteristic form of consciousness is more petty bourgeois than proletarian, even among the vast masses of workers who remain poor. They aspire to a modest prosperity and independence. The default object of desire is traditional, retrograde family business. The central economic misfortune is the squandering of this human energy, of this vast store of life, rebuffed, constrained, and diminished by lack of opportunity and instruments.

In no economy has mass production ever employed more than a small portion of the candidates for inclusion in this world of self-help and initiative. Its association with industry and its reliance on large scale as the reverse side of standardization have always prevented it from providing a solution for the majority. The knowledge economy, now known under the elitist constraints of insular and shallow vanguardism, has no such inherent constraint. Nevertheless, the path to an inclusive and deepened knowledge economy is arduous.

To tap this human energy for broad-based economic growth in the situation of a developing country, it is necessary to confront two problems—one, political and strategic; the other, conceptual and institutional. The political and strategic problem is the prejudice of the Left, whose cause such an economic project would be, against not only the small business class but also against the much larger part of the population that shares its material ambitions and moral attitudes. Instead of meeting this class on its own terms and helping it expand its conception of the forms that its dreams might take, the Left has traditionally elected the petty bourgeoisie as its enemy, with calamitous consequences in twentieth-century European history.

The conceptual and institutional problem is the need to present the actual or would-be petty bourgeois with ways of satisfying their ambitions other than the default form of isolated and backward family business. That is the agenda laid out in my earlier discussion of the legal and institutional conditions of inclusive vanguardism. This agenda begins and ends in the institutional reconstruction of the market order: at first through modest tinkering with the means of access to productive resources, then through the legal innovations shaping decentralized, pluralistic, and experimental coordination between governments and firms, and finally through a fundamental expansion and diversification of the terms on which decentralized economic agents can make use of the capital resources of society and lay claim to one another's labor.

A third point illustrated by the Brazilian example is that the institutional machinery with which to begin such a reshaping of the market order in the service of inclusive vanguardism is widely distributed, in fragmentary form throughout the world. Pieces of it exist in every major economy. It does not need to be created out of nothing. Thus, the Brazilian state and even local state governments can count on many of the entities required by the first stage of the institutional innovations that I earlier described: development banks, organizations designed to help small business upgrade its practices, entities intended to develop and transfer technology by adapting it to the conditions and the capacities for assimilation possessed by relatively backward firms in a developing country, and a quasi-governmental network of technical schools, including schools and support centers devoted to advanced manufacturing. What remains missing is a way to bring these instruments together and to enlist them in the service of the program of inclusive vanguardism. More significant than the absence of such an orchestration of forms of access is the lack of a guiding theoretical and programmatic view of the route to development after the heyday of mass production.

This dilemma of development is not a genuine dilemma at all. The first horn of the dilemma—the option of continuing along the path recommended by classical development economics and of accepting conventional mass production as the realistic horizon of achievement for a developing country—makes promises that it cannot keep. What it offers is at best a holding operation without a prospect for the future.

In the absence of a detailed view of how to approach the seemingly inaccessible goal of inclusive vanguardism, this fallback position acquires the undeserved prestige of realism: it can rely on the illusory solidity of the familiar. In the early twenty-first century, in the rich North Atlantic countries, the last-ditch defense of declining mass production against foreign and domestic competition has become a large part of the economic program of both right-wing populism and conventional social democracy. The influence of this program in the richest countries has in turn increased its prestige in the developing ones by the well-established workings of mental colonialism.

The other horn of the dilemma—the advancement of a knowledge economy for the many in the conditions of a developing country—is, for all its difficulty, the only realistic alternative. The key to implementing it is to break up the seemingly impossible task into pieces and to implement it in steps. As the presentation of the legal-institutional requirements of inclusive vanguardism has suggested, we do not need to enforce a system; we need to tread a path, revising the map along the way. Combined and uneven development along this trajectory is not only a possible way of traveling this path; it must be almost always the only one.

There is no reason to expect the opportunities to move toward such an economy to be any more limited in the major developing countries than they are in the richest economies. Compare this claim to the debate among Marx's followers about whether he was right to expect the overcoming of capitalism to happen first in the most advanced countries, and only later to spread to the rest of the world. His reasoning rested on the same assumption of a unilinear evolutionary succession of forms of economic and social organization that informed all Marx's social and economic theory. The advanced economies would be the setting appointed by history for the transition from capitalism to socialism because they and only they would have completed all the stages of the indispensable itinerary.

History did not happen that way. The transition undertaken under conditions of relative backwardness failed to conform, in outcome as well as in its process, to the model presented by the theory. Neither, however, did it follow that model in the advanced economies, as the brief experiences of revolutionary social regimes installed in Western Europe in the aftermath of the First World War showed.

What the idea of the priority of the central economies over the peripheral ones failed to acknowledge is the irreplaceable advantage of a defiant churning: of the rejection of institutional arrangements, imported from somewhere else, that failed to function as they did in the place from which they were taken and that failed to satisfy either basic needs or higher hopes. In the central economies, an openness to more fundamental alternatives turned out to be harder to achieve without the prompt of economic or military calamity. Even with that prompt, the national and transnational solidarity of elites usually proved sufficient to shut the window of historical opportunity and restore an order undisturbed by the offer of consequential alternatives.

Two forces have converged to cheat the developing countries—especially the ones that are large enough to imagine themselves as seats of resistance to the dominant interests and ideas in the world—of the opportunity to develop the knowledge economy in inclusive rather than insular form. The first force has been the weakness of democracy, either sacrificed to collective despotism or drained of its transformative potential by imitation of the constitutional arrangements of the North Atlantic societies.

The second force has been mental colonialism: the subordination of intellectual life in these countries to the currents of thought prevalent in the richest and most resigned parts of the world. The antidote to mental colonialism is not the cultivation of local heresies about development and institutions. It is the formulation and propagation of a message that is as worldwide in its destination as the message that it opposes: universalizing heresies against a universal orthodoxy. The program of inclusive vanguardism is not a luxury intended only for societies that have reached the limits of the established forms of production. It responds to a disturbing fact: the most reliable formula of economic development has stopped working everywhere.

16.

Inclusive Vanguardism and the Political Economy of the Rich Countries

Failure to develop the knowledge economy in inclusive form—or even to imagine such a development as a political-economic project—has had enormous consequences as well for the rich countries and for the positions of both the Left and the Right in their politics. We cannot understand what has happened, or what could happen, in their political life without doing justice to the influence of ideas. Technological and economic forces and class interests alone cannot explain the direction of politics in these countries or reveal how they might accelerate growth and diminish inequality.

The historical experience of these and all societies demonstrates the formative role of ideas and of the lack of them. Consider, both as an example of this role and as background to the circumstances explored in this section, the evolution of the agenda embraced in the United States and other North Atlantic societies by progressives and reformers in power from the 1930s to now.

Franklin Roosevelt and many of his collaborators were avowed and genuine experimentalists with regard to institutions and policies. The Depression and the Second World

War provided an extraordinary opportunity for the pursuit of a transformative agenda. Nevertheless, the institutional experimentalism of the early New Deal had as its organizing principle the corporatist idea of concerted action between the federal government and big business. Its overriding goal was to restabilize rather than to democratize the market order. The practice of concerted action was later resumed with a vengeance under the conditions of the war economy. In its animating assumptions about economic recovery and reconstruction as well as in the details of many of its policies for recovery and employment, the early New Deal resembled the response to the slump by other governments of the same historical period, including the Nazi regime in its early years.

Politicians and policy makers, then as now, assumed that they would have the ideas they needed when they needed them. They thought that the only obstacles with which they had to contend were those of power and interest. Both the American democrat and the German dictator remained at the mercy of the ideas available to them. To find alternatives to corporatism it was not enough to want to find them.

In the evolution of the New Deal, the corporatist impulse gave way to a narrower focus on crafting safeguards against economic insecurity. (The Social Security program was the most important example.) The provision of antidotes to economic insecurity was in turn followed, after the war and the war economy, by policies designed to support mass consumption. The turn to mass consumption relied on the expansion of debt and credit, on stark imbalances between surplus and deficit economies, and on countercyclical management of the economy in the spirit of popular Keynesianism.

Throughout each step of this trajectory, the same assumptions remained in place. According to these assumptions, the state can regulate the market economy more intensively and soften its inequalities after the fact by use of progressive taxation and social spending. What it cannot do is to reinvent the constitutive institutional and legal arrangements of a market regime. These arrangements are what they are.

Thinking that is useful to the advancement of an inclusive form of the knowledge economy must challenge these assumptions. Prominent among the conditions of such an alternative are its legal-institutional requirements, understood as a pathway rather than as a blueprint or a system. The pathway begins with initiatives that form part of the established stock of policy ideas. But it moves toward innovations in the legal regimes of property and of employment. Such innovations do more than increase or diminish the space of the market vis-à-vis the state. They put one market order in the place of another.

This history of ideas and of experience helps explain the shape of discourse in contemporary politics and political economy. For some time the dominant project of the governing elites in North America and Western Europe has been the reconciliation of American-style economic flexibility with European-style social protection within a barely adjusted version of the inherited economic institutions and laws.

The commanding agenda at the center of national politics in many of these societies has been to make social democracy more "flexible," in the name of fairness as well as of efficiency, while making liberalism more "social." The chief way to liberalize social democracy has been to amend labor laws that protect insiders and incumbents in the stable, capital-intensive part of the labor market to the detriment of the unemployed and to those in unstable or precarious employment. It has also been to design social and economic rights so that they are universal and portable rather than dependent on holding any particular job.

The principal proposal to make liberalism social has been to enhance guarantees against economic insecurity in proportion to gains in the flexibility of labor markets. This proposal has often remained an unfulfilled promise. Its fulfillment would require a well-financed state acting (as it often did in the North Atlantic countries in the thirty years from 1945 to 1975) against the background of rapid economic growth. Such growth would require a sustained rise in productivity made possible by the economy-wide diffusion of the most advanced practice of production. To liberalize social democracy without making liberalism social by enhancing economic opportunity and empowerment and combating precarious employment is to hollow social democracy out, turning the vaunted synthesis into a de facto retreat.

The absence of an inclusive form of the knowledge economy as a living and influential idea, not just as a still-distant economic and political achievement, has helped shape politics and policy in the rich countries of today on the Right and the Left as well as in the Center. It has done so indirectly by its consequences for economic stagnation and inequality. It has done so directly by its effect on assumptions about alternatives to the present course of economic policy and economic growth. The lack of such an alternative in doctrine as well as in practice has exercised as powerful an influence as was the influence of a dearth of developed alternatives to corporatist concerted action between government and business in the crisis of the 1930s.

To the left of the social-democratic and social-liberal Center that I have described is a Left that has lost faith in the governmental direction of the economy but that recognizes the inadequacy of institutionally conservative social democracy and of its liberalization as a way to fulfill the historical goals of progressives. To the right of that Center, and of its program of liberalizing social democracy and of making liberalism social, is a rightwing populism. It seeks to win the allegiance of a working-class majority whose troubles and aspirations the project of the Center has failed to solve or even to address.

Consider the shared assumptions of this Right and this Left and the way in which their dispute would be transformed by recognition of the alternative of inclusive vanguardism.

First, both these forces continue to assume, as did classic or conservative liberals and Marxists alike, from the nineteenth century onward, that the market economy, or "capitalism," has an inbuilt legal and institutional architecture, open to only a limited range of variation, such as the differences studied in the literature about "varieties of capitalism." This shared assumption already excludes the program of inclusive vanguardism, which requires, for its development beyond its initial steps, innovation in arrangements as fundamental as those that define the property regime and the legal form of free labor, as well as the terms on which the state—or decentralized entities that it sets up— can work with firms and firms can work with one another.

Second, as contemporary progressives and rightwing populists envision no alternative market regime, they can have no transformative approach to the supply side of the economy. Progressives have largely abandoned the supply side to conservatives and resigned themselves to the primacy of demand-oriented policies. The supply-side project of populist as well as traditional (classical-liberal or neoliberal) conservatives has been the preservation or restoration of a market order whose legal and institutional content they take to be self-evident. They misrepresent any attempt to reshape economic institutions as governmental intervention in the economy and fail to distinguish between suppressing the market and remaking it. They cannot, or will not, imagine the existence of a different market regime.

Third, in the absence of structural alternatives, this Left and this Right resign themselves to defending belated industrial mass production rather than working toward its conversion to advanced manufacturing and its associated services—the form taken by the knowledge economy in those parts of economic life. Sweetheart deals with businesses that threaten to leave the country or downsize as well as restraints on trade form part of the same orientation.

It is one thing to support traditional mass production as a way to play for time in the course of an effort to turn it into its more advanced successor. It is another thing to use the afterlife of Fordist manufacturing as a surrogate for the missing alternative. That is a policy of desperation, without a future, for the same reasons that it no longer has a future in the developing countries notwithstanding the authority that classical development economics continues to enjoy.

Fourth, this Left and this Right acquiesce in the use of easy-money policy (expansionary monetary policy implemented by the central bank) as their default strategy of economic growth. The fiscal constraints on governmental initiative reduce the role of expansionary fiscal policy and the prospects for massive public investment—notably in the physical infrastructure of economy. Easy money, however, cannot replace the missing strategy of economic growth; its powers to stimulate growth and employment are soon exhausted.

The differences between this Left and this Right with respect to the reach of regulation of economic activity, the level, financing, and redistributive character of public services and social entitlements, the virtues of progressive taxation, and even the use of public resources and governmental initiative to develop new technologies are real. However, they come down to matters of degree in the formulation and implementation of policy. The shared assumptions in practical political economy that I have enumerated limit the significance of these differences. They renew the life of the centrist project of combining economic flexibility with social protection, of liberalizing social democracy and of making liberalism social even as failure to secure socially inclusive economic growth erodes their appeal.

This diminishment of the horizon of politics and of practical political economy has a historical background that illuminates its significance: the social-democratic settlement of the mid-twentieth century and the failure of the Center, Left, and Right positions that I described to reopen the terms of that compromise. We can understand this settlement as a bargain, presaged in the troubled period preceding the Second World War and worked out in the first three decades after the war. Under the terms of this bargain, the forces that sought to change the organization of production and power renounced this challenge (or were confined to the margins of national politics when they failed to renounce it). In return, the state was allowed to gain the power to regulate the economy more intensively, to attenuate economic inequalities by means of progressive taxation and social spending, and to smooth economic instability through the use of counter-cyclical monetary and fiscal policy. The abandonment of any attempt to reimagine and to remake the market order became more than an idea; it was built into the institutions and the practices as well as the most influential political and economic doctrines in these countries. It defined the institutional and ideological context of the centrist, progressive, and conservative positions that I have described. Their premises derived from its assumptions.

None of the fundamental problems of the contemporary societies, however, can be solved or even addressed within the institutional and ideological terms of this settlement. To address them and to solve them requires us to reopen the terms of the social-democratic compromise by innovating in our economic and political institutions. We would have to do so, however, in the only way in which structural change is ordinarily possible, piece by piece and step by step. It does not happen as a wholesale substitution of one predefined institutional system by another in the manner imagined by the radical programmatic agendas of the nineteenth and twentieth centuries.

Among these problems is the hierarchical segmentation of the economy between advanced and backward sectors. This segmentation denies to the majority of workers and firms the means to be more productive and destroys the basis for socially inclusive economic growth. The failure of the social-democratic compromise, in either its historical or updated, liberalized form, to solve this and other problems of the advanced societies leads to the frustration so salient in their present political life: the conviction of the working-class majority that its interests and aspirations have been sacrificed.

Here lies the significance of the program of inclusive vanguardism for the richest countries in the world. This program can offer a response to economic stagnation and inequality only because its assumptions as well as its proposals contrast with those of the centrist, leftwing, and rightwing positions that I have described. It reopens the terms of the mid-twentieth-century settlement by insisting on what that settlement excluded: the attempt to reshape the arrangements defining the market rather than just to give the market and the state more or less play relative to each other.

Viewed in this context, inclusive vanguardism is more than an idea about the economy. It forms part of a position in politics and practical political economy. It is the first and most important of three connected themes that compose the core content of such a political economy. The other two themes are the relation of finance to the real economy and the relation of labor to capital.

Finance should be a good servant rather than a bad master. It should serve the productive agenda of society rather than being allowed to serve itself. The funding of the creation of new assets in new ways, now a small part of the activity of the capital market, should become a major part. The knowledge economy requires capital-intensive radical innovations, not just efficiency-enhancing, capital-sparing initiatives.

We can move in this direction by both negative and positive means. We can move negatively by discouraging financial activity that makes no colorable contribution to the expansion of output and the enhancement of productivity. We can move positively by creating arrangements that channel capital to production, especially to the creation of new assets in new ways, and combine access to capital with access to advanced technology, practice, and knowledge.

The pursuit of higher productivity outside the insular vanguards to which the knowledge economy remains confined also requires a sequence of institutional and legal innovations strengthening the position of labor in its relation to capital. An upward tilt to the returns to labor has historically been a nearly indispensable condition of sustained progress in making productivity-enhancing innovations. Moreover, the empowerment of labor prevents the economic potential of a more widely disseminated version of the most advanced practice of production from being sacrificed to the financial interests of asset owners and the power interests of managers. A deepened and widespread knowledge economy thrives in the setting of free labor: the freer, the better.

My discussion of the legal-institutional requirements of an inclusive knowledge economy began to explore their implications for the relation between capital and labor. In the short term, we must prevent the reorganization of production, on the basis of decentralized contractual arrangements and of labor and tax arbitrage in the world economy, from consigning an increasing part of the labor force to precarious employment. We need to create, alongside the established labor laws, responsive to the circumstances of industrial mass production (private employment) and administrative Fordism (public employment), a second body of labor laws to master the new realities of production. This second set of labor laws would provide for the organization and representation of workers in these once anomalous situations of part-time, temporary, and subcontracted work, or of involuntary self-employment undertaken as a form of wage work without the guarantees and benefits that wage labor may enjoy. When these workers cannot be adequately organized and represented, or the results of organization and representation remain inadequate, the law would intervene directly in the employment relation to protect the precarious worker. The most important form of protection would be a legal requirement of price neutrality: work performed under these conditions would have to be paid at least as much as the closest equivalent work rendered under a regime of stable, full-time employment.

Over the long term, labor becomes freer as economically dependent wage labor gives way to the higher forms of free labor: self-employment and cooperation or partnership. Self-employment and cooperation cannot become the leading varieties of free labor unless they can be reconciled with the imperative of the large-scale aggregation of resources. They cannot be reconciled with that imperative without innovation in the terms of decentralized access to the resources and opportunities of production, which is to say in the regimes of property and contract. The traditional unified property right must become only one of several ways to organize decentralized economic initiative. Alternative regimes of private law—of property and contract—must come to coexist experimentally within the same market economy.

The establishment of a disseminated and radicalized form of the knowledge economy, the reshaping of the relation of finance to the real economy the better to enlist finance in the service of production, and the progress of free work toward its higher forms of self-employment and cooperation, beginning with the protection of precarious labor, form the heart of an alternative to institutionally conservative social democracy and social liberalism. They define the main axes of an economic agenda that can do what the social-democratic settlement of the mid-twentieth century, in its contemporary liberalized form, is no longer able to accomplish: to lay the basis for a sustained, broad-based rise in productivity and to address the inequalities resulting from the hierarchical segmentation of the economy. To advance beyond its initial steps such a political economy must draw on the other changes in society, politics, and culture discussed in earlier parts of the argument of this book.

First, this agenda in practical political economy relies, for the capabilities that it requires, on schooling that sides with the mind as imagination against the mind as machine and encyclopedia. It depends on a strengthening of experimentalism in every sphere of culture, even in domains that seem to be remote from economic activity. In the absence of this wider cultural change, the predominant character of our experience, with its restraints on discovery, will threaten to override and weaken the program of economic reconstruction.

Second, it needs to develop rather than to abandon the greatest legacy of historical social democracy: its investment in people and their capabilities. To do so, it should not and need not resign itself to the choice between administrative Fordism (the bureaucratic provision of standardized public services) and the contracting of public services to profit-driven firms. It needs to engage civil society in partnering with government, through a range of forms of cooperative activity, to provide those services. It is not enough to reshape economic and political institutions. We must also innovate in the institutional and legal forms of the relation of the state to civil society.

Third, it calls for a high-energy democracy that can subject the established structure of society, including its arrangements for the organization of the market and for the disposition of public services, to pressure and testing. Such a democracy dispenses with crisis as the condition of change and makes structural change a commonplace extension of our ordinary experience. It allows us to change the formative arrangements and assumptions of the society and the economy in piecemeal and stepwise form. It does so under political institutions that raise the temperature and hasten the pace of politics.

A deepened and disseminated knowledge economy, a dialectical education, the self-construction of civil society through its partnering with the state in the provision of public services, and a high-energy democracy are reciprocally reinforcing projects. Failure to progress in any of them may limit our progress in all the others. They form, however, no system: circumstance and choice must determine on which front or fronts we advance first before hitting against the constraints imposed by failure to advance on the other fronts.

In this process of combined and uneven development, the program of inclusive vanguardism plays a major role. All our moral as well as our material interests become harder to achieve in a context of relative economic stagnation and disempowerment. In such a context we deny to the majority of ordinary men and women a chance to share in the experience, the powers, and the rewards of the most advanced practice of production.

Once we begin to think and to act along these lines, we are compelled to reinterpret the relation among Left, Right, and Center in politics. We no longer need the form of political thinking and action that has been called populism, with its illusory extra-institutional shortcut to the fulfillment of popular grievances. We connect our material interest in economic growth and in the development of our productive powers with our moral interest in the enhancement of agency: our power to act, to innovate, and to turn the tables, as individuals and as peoples organized under the protection of states, on the established arrangements of the economy and the state.

17.

Growth, Crisis, and Successive Breakthroughs of the Constraints on Supply and Demand: The Larger Economic Meaning of Inclusive Vanguardism

The enigma of supply and demand

Consider now the significance of the widespread knowledge economy not for the practical prospects of developing countries and of the richest economies in the world but for the most rudimentary feature of economic life: the relation between supply and demand. What seems clear and simple is in fact obscure and enigmatic. To grasp the bearing of inclusive vanguardism on the relation between supply and demand is to develop our understanding of the significance for economic growth and crisis of a knowledge economy in which many share.

The main line of economic thinking, at least since the marginalist turn of the late nineteenth century, teaches that supply and demand will adjust to each other in the absence of flaws in the workings of the market. Each such flaw amounts to a departure from perfect competition. In the absence of such imperfections, supply and demand will come into balance. The process by which they adjust to each other ensures that resources, including our most precious resource, our time, human labor, will be devoted to their most efficient uses.

The particular sources of supply and demand are, according to this way of thinking, irrelevant to an understanding of the basic and universal mechanism by which supply and demand adjust to each other. Whatever the source of supply or of demand, they will adjust until eventually they reach equilibrium, unless a failure of perfect competition (in any of its dimensions including information as well as market power) prevents them from doing so. Under this view, we imagine both supply and demand as homogenous and continuous quantities, facilitating their mathematical representation. We can then distinguish the mathematical analysis of their reciprocal adjustment from the explanation of what causes each of them to expand or contract. We can assign these causal inquiries to separate branches of economics, especially the theory of economic growth and the study of the business cycle, or more generally (if such a discipline existed) of economic crisis.

I suggest a different way of thinking about supply and demand and of inclusive vanguardism. This way of thinking makes explicit some of the assumptions underlying my approach to the knowledge economy and to its futures. In this book I cannot hope to demonstrate the superiority of this view, only to show how it allows us to make better sense of many aspects of economic history that have remained unexplained. Among these aspects are those that have to do with the evolution and present state of the knowledge economy.

As with any general view, the one that I sketch admits of no direct empirical refutation. It does not follow that it is invulnerable to empirical challenge. It has a broad periphery of implications about matters of fact. On that periphery, it is falsifiable.

Here are five ideas that compose this way of thinking.

The first idea is that economic growth requires successive breakthroughs in the constraints on both supply and demand. For growth to persist, an advance on the demand side of the economy must be met by a corresponding advance on the supply side and vice versa. Of course, the dominant approach to supply and demand incorporates the same idea. However, it represents the correspondence of advances on the supply and the demand sides of the economy to be automatic, except if a specific market imperfection prevents it from happening.

All of this may seem too obvious to mention except for a problem that escapes notice so long as we remain in the grip of the prevailing account of supply and demand. If more supply generated more demand, and more demand provoked more supply, the reciprocal adjustment of supply and demand should lead to perpetual economic growth. It would do so even in the absence of technological and organizational innovations that raise productivity, except if the constraint of diminishing marginal returns (heretofore the most plausible candidate for the role of a universal law of economic life) sufficed to account for economic stagnation.

The second idea is that breakthroughs of the constraints on supply and on demand are discontinuous. There are different ways of expanding both supply and demand.

Each of them has its own logic: its mode of operation, its potential, and its limits. These distinctive ways of sustaining expansion on the demand or the supply side of the economy have differing reach, efficacy, and staying power. Some are shallower and more short-lived than others. Some quickly exhaust themselves; others go further toward being self-sustaining. They do so because they have a more transformative effect on economic institutions and practices as well as on the capabilities of economic agents.

We can arrange the modes of expansion of demand and of supply in a hierarchy. There is no direct or spontaneous passage from one mode to the next more powerful one, as if exhausting the potential of one of these modes of expansion guaranteed passage to the next. This lack of automatic passage from one basis for increasing supply or demand to the next, hierarchically superior, one is what I mean by calling the expansion of supply and demand discontinuous. We are driven to take notice of this discontinuity when we refuse to separate, as the ruling ideas do, the short-term vicissitudes of supply and demand from the causes of economic growth and stagnation.

I later outline and rank, in the inverse order of their potential to sustain economic growth, these different bases for the reciprocal adjustment of supply and demand. Each is more promising than the one before it in turning the reciprocal adjustment of supply and demand into the outward, visible expression of a mechanism of economic growth.

The third idea is that breakthroughs of the constraints on demand and on supply are heteronomous. By this I mean that no automatic correspondence exists between an advance from one basis for the expansion of demand or supply and a corresponding advance on the other side, of supply or demand. It does not follow from an advance in supporting demand, from one basis for such an advance to another basis (for example, from increasing purchasing power by encouraging household debt to increasing it through progressive taxation and social spending), that we will achieve a corresponding advance on the supply side of the economy (for example, from an expansion of supply without productivity-enhancing innovations to one with them).

The heteronomy of the reciprocal adjustment of supply and demand aggravates the consequence of its discontinuity. Discontinuity is unilateral: it is about the failure of automatic passage from one basis for the expansion of demand or supply to the next, more effective or transformative basis. Heteronomy is bilateral: it is about the inability of such an advance on one side of the economy (demand or supply) to guarantee an advance on the other side.

The fourth idea is that the discontinuity and the heteronomy of the reciprocal adjustment of demand and supply are the primary basis of economic instability. The fundamental reason for the susceptibility of economic growth to breakdown is the nonexistence of what the dominant way of thinking assumes to be fact: that in the absence of a market imperfection, supply and demand will adjust to each other, ensuring the assignment of resources and labor to their most efficient uses.

If failure of spontaneous correspondence between the expansion of supply and the expansion of demand is the first basis of economic instability, its secondary basis is the fraught and variable relation of finance to the real economy. In the next part of this section, I comment on the aspect of this relation to which Keynes gave such great emphasis: money matters. The liquidity of money balances, disengaged from particular productive activities, allows them to serve as the pliant instrument of our impulses of fear and greed, despondency and hope. However, this kidnapping of money by our humors is only a sideline to a more fundamentally unsettling aspect of the relation of finance to the real economy.

Just as there is no single natural and necessary way of organizing a market regime, so too is there no single natural and necessary way of arranging one of the aspects of such a regime—the relation of finance to the real economy. Different ways of organizing a market economy can tighten or loosen the relation of finance to the real economy. The looser the connection, and the more the transactions of the real economy become pretexts for financial activity rather than its genuine concern, the greater the risk that finance will do harm.

Under the arrangements now established in the rich economies, the production system is largely self-financed. The funding of production relies mainly on the retained and reinvested earnings of firms: hence on financing generated within the production system itself. The creation of new assets in new ways—the concern of venture capital and related forms of finance—accounts for a minute part of financial activity. Even initial or secondary public offerings represent a relatively small portion of finance. Under these arrangements finance threatens to become a bad master rather than a good servant.

The theory of economic instability or crisis is just the reverse side of the theory of economic growth: it deals with the susceptibility of growth to disruption. And the understanding of how supply and demand accommodate to each other dynamically, in time, is simply one way of addressing, over the short term, the problems of growth and instability.

The fifth idea is that if we travel far enough up the hierarchy of ways of overcoming the constraints on the expansion of supply and of demand to the more far-reaching and more lasting ways of superseding those constraints, we eventually come to a class of solutions that do expand demand by the same means through which they increase supply: an institutionalized broadening of access to the resources, opportunities, and capabilities of production. At this point, and only at this point, that which increases demand also increases supply. What the prevalent way of thinking supposes to be the natural state of economic life—the reciprocal accommodation of supply and demand—is in fact a characteristic of exceptional varieties of economic organization: those that have the property of breaching the limits of both supply and demand by equipping more economic agents with the means and occasions for productive initiative.

The sixth idea is that there exists an especially potent and promising subset of the circumstances represented by the fifth idea: this subset breaches the constraints on both supply and demand by broadening access to the most advanced practice of production. On the supply side, such initiatives increase the number of those who can share in the work of the most productive parts of the economy. On the demand side, they put people in a position to claim, as wealth creators, not simply as beneficiaries of retrospective and compensatory redistribution, a share in the wealth that they have helped produce.

If this most advanced practice of production is the knowledge economy, the potential for the expansion of both supply and demand is especially great. The knowledge economy offers admission to a form of productive activity that tends to make innovation perpetual and that promises to relax or reverse the rule of diminishing marginal returns to an increasing input in the process of production.

Henry Ford once quipped that he liked to pay his workers well so that they could buy his cars. They could have used the money to buy other things, or to buy cars made by his competitors. There is no contractual solution to the problem evoked by Ford's remark. There is only an institutional solution.

An inclusive vanguardism—the developed and widespread form of the knowledge economy—is now that solution. It puts paid to the unnaturalness of the reciprocal accommodation of supply and demand. By giving new shape to the market economy, it results in what the dominant ideas about supply and demand mistakenly assume to happen automatically unless imperfect competition prevents it from happening.

Contrast to Keynes's teaching

The way of thinking about supply and demand that I have just outlined stands in contrast to Keynes's economic theory, especially as formulated in his *General Theory of Employment, Interest and Money* (1936). The prompt for Keynes's work, which formulated the most influential economic heresy of the twentieth century, was the economic breakdown of the 1930s. Its central theme was the way in which supply and demand may fail to adjust until they come into balance at a low level of employment and activity. It was thus similar to the view that I have just sketched in that it gave reason to disbelieve that the market economy, as it was then or is now constituted, would correct itself and perform its expected role of assigning all resources to their most efficient uses. To assign all resources, including labor, to their most efficient uses, it would have to maintain full employment.

One way to mark how the approach that I have just sketched differs from Keynes's view is to suggest in what ways Keynes's doctrine—and the policy prescriptions to which it gave rise—are deficient from the perspective of the proposed alternative.

The first limitation of Keynes's view is that it offers a theory of a special case: one of the many ways in which supply and demand may fail to adjust, or adjust only at a diminished level of employment and activity. The special case that Keynes theorized was one violating Say's law: supply would fail to create its own demand. A failure to translate saving into productive investment (thus hoarding), made possible by the inflexibility of a particular price (the downward rigidity of wages, studied by Marshall and his disciple Pigou), could result in a failure to sustain aggregate demand. The effect of our unstable humors, of elation or despondency, on the disposition of liquid money balances could magnify and prolong the slump: what began as a failure of confidence might end as a decline in real economy activity for which there would be no spontaneous mechanism of correction. Government would then have to make up by fiscal policy, or direct public spending and initiative, the deficient demand and restart the economy.

Here was an account and a theory of one way in which supply and demand may fail to adjust to each other, or come into balance only at a depressed level of activity. There are many other ways, already implied even in the rudimentary and abstract outline presented in the preceding pages. We know from Keynes's own occasional writings in the years before the *General Theory* that he considered other responses to the crisis of the time and other ways of understanding it. However, he chose to characterize the slump by emphasizing insufficient demand (rather than, for example, inadequate investment) for reasons that may have been more strategic and political than substantive and theoretical: a response suggesting governmental influence on the investment decision was, to his eyes, less palatable politically and therefore less capable of implementation than one that blamed inadequate demand and required expansionary fiscal policy as an antidote.

From 2007 to 2009 the United States and other advanced economies underwent a financial crisis, followed by a sharp decline in real economic activity. If this disturbance was not as serious as the economic collapse with which Keynes and his contemporaries dealt in the 1930s, it nevertheless exceeded the dimension of the standard "business cycle" of the time. And although it evoked the standard response of fiscal stimulus and expansionary monetary policy (the latter, contrary to the spirit of Keynes's prescriptions, even more than the former), it was soon recognized as a breakdown different in character and causation, if not in consequence, from the one that had faced Keynes. Some described it as a "balance-sheet recession," in which exorbitant household and corporate debt triggered financial instability that later contaminated the real economy.

The United States had stopped making enough goods and services that the rest of the world wanted. For several decades, there had been a sharply regressive redistribution of income and wealth. It had been compensated by an extravagant expansion of debt and credit, especially for households, underwritten by the residual strategy of economic growth in the United States, the policy of cheap money, as well as by trade and capital deficits, especially in the commercial and financial dealings of the US with China. By the very nature of its immediate causes, this slump required, even more evidently than had the more extreme crisis of the 1930s, action on the supply side of the economy. It therefore called for what Keynes's doctrine was not, despite the title of his masterwork: a general theory of the failures of reciprocal adjustment of supply and demand.

A second limitation of Keynes's theory was its lack of structural content or institutional vision. Although intended as apostasy, it exaggerated one of the most characteristic features of the tradition of English political economy: its subordination of institutions to psychology in its preferred explanations. The key categories in Keynes's system—the preference for liquidity, the propensity to consume, and the state of long-term expectations—are all psychological. Our impulses lead us to dispose of liquid money balances one way or the other and through this disposition exercise decisive influence on the direction of the real economy.

There is a close relation between the predominance of the psychological over the institutional and the focus on the demand side of the economy to the detriment of attention to the supply side. There is also a relation between the psychologism of Keynes's doctrine and its view—consistent with the marginalist tradition—of economics as a theory of market-based exchange to the prejudice of economics as a theory of production.

Consider the matter from the revealing standpoint of the practical response to a decline in employment and economic activity. It is as least possible to deal with an inadequacy of what Keynes called aggregate demand by committing public funds, or using governmental policy to influence private spending, without any change in the institutional arrangements of the economy or the organization of the production. More effective action on the demand side of the economy requires structural change: institutional innovations that reshape the primary distribution of economic advantage by broadening access to economic opportunities and capabilities. But at least it is possible to imagine a way of addressing a deficiency of demand that avoids any such attempt to bring about structural change. The possibility of dispensing with it was one of the features that attracted Keynes and his followers to the demand-oriented focus of their view and of their policy proposals.

We cannot allow ourselves to foreswear interest in the institutions of the market and the arrangements of production when we find the causes of a slump to lie on the supply side of the economy as well as on its demand side. Action on the supply side of the economy is by necessity structural action. It is structural even if its aim, as has traditionally been the case with conservative or neoliberal economic policy in the rich North Atlantic countries, has been to restore a supposedly canonical version of the market economy to its pure or purer form rather than to reform economic institutions.

A third defect of Keynes's view results from the other two. It is an unfinished theory because it is a truncated one, mistaking a special case for a general account and dealing with problems that are ultimately structural without having a structural vision. It is more than a theory of how supply and demand may come into equilibrium at a level of activity that underutilizes labor and the other resources of the economy. But it is less than a theory of perennial disequilibrium in the economy—a susceptibility to breakdown that can be brought to an end, I argue, only by the structural transformation that I here label inclusive vanguardism.

It cannot be such a theory on account of the first two limitations that I have described. For one thing, it is not a general theory. It attaches decisive weight to factors, such as the downward rigidity of wages or the disposition to hoard, that will be much more important in some circumstances than in others, according to the institutional and legal arrangements governing, for example, the relative powers of labor and capital and the place of finance in the real economy as well as the more intangible variations of the culture and consciousness of economic agents.

For another thing, it is bereft of any vision of the alternative ways of organizing a market economy. As a consequence, it lacks a criterion by which to distinguish the ways of organizing an economy, on the supply as well as the demand side, that are more or less likely to lead to breakdowns in real economic activity—the breakdowns that the reciprocal adjustment of supply and demand is unable spontaneously to overcome.

In such a theory there is no basis for saying that the economy is either naturally susceptible to a failure in the reciprocal adjustment of supply and demand or not. It is possible to say only that at any moment, given certain specific assumptions (e.g., about the power of labor to defend the wage against reductions, the power of capitalists to control investment decisions, and the power of savers to withhold saving from productive investment), full employment may not be reached because of a foreseeable combination of circumstances. For this combination, there exists a specific remedy.

By contrast, in the view that I outline here the economy remains in perpetual disequilibrium—supply and demand fail to adjust to each other and to provide a mechanism for repeated breakthroughs of the constraints on supply and demand—until something happens. That something is in no sense natural. It is the product of a long economic evolution and requires, to be completed, a change in the institutions by which we organize a decentralized economy as well as in its practices of production. To this change I give the name inclusive vanguardism.

The spectrum of breakthroughs in the constraints on demand

There is a spectrum of ways to break through the constraints on the expansion of demand. Each level of breakthrough has greater potential than the one before to persist and to contribute to a self-reinforcing cycle of economic growth. Each has its own logic and its own limitations. There is never a direct and spontaneous passage from one to the next: that is the import of the characteristic discontinuity among levels of breakthrough. Nor does any movement up this ladder ensure a corresponding movement up the ladder of discontinuous advances on the supply side of the economy—the feature of heteronomy. Only at the far end of the spectrum—or at the top of the ladder—is there a deep and reliable basis for what, according to the dominant ideas, is supposed naturally to happen in the absence of a market failure: a way of breaching the demand constraints that also overcomes the supply constraints on economic growth.

The first level is expansion of demand through an increase of indebtedness—of firms but especially of households—without any change, other than through this rise in leverage, in the distribution of income and wealth. The chief instrument for such an increase and popularization of credit may be expansionary monetary policy, which in the United States as in many economies has increasingly served as the default strategy of economic growth, wielded by the central bank rather than by the federal government. It is a sign of desperation—the desperation of the lack of apparent alternatives other than fiscal stimulus—that this instrument has continued to be used despite mounting evidence of its ineffectiveness and its dangers.

A telling example of how this way of expanding demand comes to be adopted as well as of its inadequacy is the American experience in the years that preceded the financial and economic crisis of 2007–2009. Franklin Roosevelt's New Deal went through three stages in its evolution between the crisis of the 1930s and the end of the Second World War. It had passed through an early period of institutional experimentation, narrowly focused, despite Roosevelt's boldness, on restabilization of the economy and corporatist management or contain-ment of competition. It had subsequently narrowed its focus to the provision of antidotes to economic insecu-rity (of which the Social Security program came to be the iconic example). And in the astonishing episode of the war economy, it had designed, under pressure of national emergency, a radical departure from the economic arrangements and ideology that were supposedly sacro-sanct in the country. It had combined this practical, untheorized, and immensely successful heresy with a massive mobilization of national resources. Once the war had ended, postwar administrations turned to what earlier stages of the New Deal's itinerary had already prefigured: the development of mass consumption as both a driver of economic growth and the most tangible practical outcome of the effort to democratize the economy on the demand side.

From the 1970s onward, however, the United States and other rich economies underwent a sharply regressive redistribution of income and wealth that was in principle incompatible with the development of a market in mass-consumption goods. Debt, facilitated by expansionary monetary policy and by trade and capital deficits with the surplus economies, helped resolve the contradiction—superficially, temporarily, and at a high cost. The financial troubles of 2008 and the subsequent economic slump revealed the magnitude of that cost.

To be sustained, an expansion of the economy powered by debt and credit has to find a basis in what I next describe as the deeper ways of breaking through constraints on the demand side of the economy as well as in a loosening of constraints on the supply side. A credit-and-debt-driven expansion cannot be a substitute for such breakthroughs.

A second level of ways of breaking through the constraints on demand is the moderation of inequality of wealth and income by retrospective, compensatory redistribution through progressive taxation and public spending on social entitlements and transfers. The increase of purchasing power by such corrective redistribution creates a basis of expansion that is more far-reaching and self-sustaining than one that relies solely on the popularization of credit. However, it is less self-sustaining than a sequence of cumulative institutional and policy innovations that broaden and democratize demand by influencing the primary distribution of income and wealth: the distribution that is generated by the market order as that order is currently organized.

The effects of this way of overcoming constraints on the expansion of demand are limited, and the conditions for achieving these outcomes are stringent. The effects are limited because they work at cross-purposes to the institutions and incentives established by the present form of the market. As the retrospective redistribution becomes more consequential and begins substantially to modify the distribution of advantage that the established market regime both presupposes and reproduces, it also starts to contradict the incentive message of existing economic arrangements. At some point, it begins to disorganize those arrangements. In practice redistribution almost never crosses this threshold: the threshold beyond which "equity" undermines "efficiency."

There is a significant qualification to this barrier imposed on the efficacy of compensatory redistribution through progressive taxation and social spending by its antagonism to the effects of established institutional arrangements and assumptions. This qualification results from an ambiguity in the relation between compensatory redistribution and the reshaping of the arrangements that define the primary distribution of economic advantage. To the extent that the use of redistributive social spending becomes investment in people and their skills, it crosses the divide between the second and the third levels of expansion; it shares in the character of a broadening of access to opportunities and capabilities and consequently of change in the initial distribution. As a result, its transformative reach extends farther.

To use corrective redistribution by tax and transfer effectively, we need to obey three principles invoked earlier in the argument of this book. These principles put such redistribution in its place, allowing it its proper subsidiary role. By their seemingly paradoxical character and their preference for higher transformative ambitions, they run counter to the ideas and attitudes that have ordinarily guided the redistributive practice of social democrats and social liberals.

The first principle is that retrospective redistribution is always subsidiary to change in the institutions shaping the primary distribution of economic advantage: the distribution resulting from the workings of the market before the correction. The limitations of tax-and-transfer can be overcome only by innovations in the institutional framework of the market economy, just as the limitations of growth on the basis of leverage can be overcome only by change in the distribution of economic advantage—superficially through compensatory redistribution and then more consequentially through structural change. This interpretation of the first principle shows how it fits together with the idea of a hierarchy of ways of breaking through demand-side constraints on economic growth.

The second principle is that with regard to the internal composition of tax-and-transfer, in the performance of its subsidiary role, the aggregate level of the tax take and the redistributive effects of public spending matter more than the progressive profile of taxation. A tax that is neutral in its impact on relative prices and admittedly regressive in its redistributive consequences may raise the most public revenue with the least disruption of established economic arrangements and incentives. The tax take may then be spent in ways that more than compensate for the regressive profile of taxation. This implicit exchange of regressivity for progressivity has been central to the practice, as distinct from the doctrine, of social democracy and social liberalism: the regressive and indirect taxation of consumption has financed a high level of social entitlements.

The third principle is that the tax system may nevertheless be designed to perform a useful but subsidiary redistributive role. Its chief target is the hierarchy of standards of living, manifested in individualized consumption. And the best way for tax to perform this role is to tax on a steeply progressive scale the difference between the total income of the individual—including returns to capital as well as to labor—and his invested saving. That difference is what he takes out of the accumulated capital of society and spends on himself.

The second and third principles express even more clearly the significance of the truth stated by the first principle: in the diminishment of inequality as in the organization of broad-based and socially inclusive economic growth, innovation in the institutional arrangements of the economy trumps both credit expansion and corrective, after-the-fact redistribution.

These principles have been observed only rarely and in fragmentary form. And when respected, they have been followed without the benefit of supporting ideas that can elucidate, at once and as a whole, the problems that they address. The consequence has been to make compensatory redistribution—the second-tier expansion of demand— even less effective than it needs to be.

Having addressed the expansion of credit and compensatory redistribution by tax and transfer, I now come to the third and most powerful and lasting basis on which to overcome the demand constraints on economic growth: the development of institutional innovations that broaden access to the resources, opportunities, and capabilities of production. Through this broadening, such innovations influence the distribution of advantage—educational as well as economic—before any measure of corrective redistribution by means of progressive taxes and social entitlements and transfers has done its work.

Here, for the first time, in the ascent up the ladder of encouragements to the expansion of demand the initiatives that breach demand-side constraints on economic growth also overcome supply-side constraints. This third level of actions has a twofold advantage over the ways of expanding demand discussed earlier. The first advantage is that they are more far-reaching and sustainable. Instead of contradicting established economic arrangements and the incentives to which those arrangements give rise, they reorder the arrangements and redirect the incentives. The second advantage is that unlike the previous two levels of initiatives, they are not confined to the demand side. They touch the supply as well as the demand side of the economy and do so by the same chain of causes and effects.

The institutional innovations that created the setting for entrepreneurial family-scale agriculture in the United States in the first half of the nineteenth century provide a canonical example. In the decades following independence and preceding the Civil War, Americans resisted a thesis that was embraced by both business elites and Marxists in the course of the nineteenth century: that agrarian concentration—with the formation of large landholdings and the expulsion of smallholders from the countryside—was intrinsic to the development of "capitalism."

The federal and state governments did much more than distribute public lands to families ready to till them. They acted to organize the institutional machinery and economic instruments of efficient, market-oriented agriculture, especially on the agrarian frontier and in the parts of the United States that had rid themselves of the incubus of slavery. In today's vocabulary, we would describe the institutional framework that they created as decentralized strategic coordination between the federal and local governments and the farmers and cooperative competition among the farmers. These efforts included, in the form of the land-grant colleges, the establishment of the intellectual basis of an agriculture that even at relatively small scale could benefit fully from the most advanced science of the time. It also enlisted economic and legal tools, such as minimal price supports, food stockpiles, and crop or income insurance, that could safeguard family-scale agriculture against the consequences of the combination of economic and physical risk: price volatility and climate volatility.

Such efforts exemplified, as had programs of agrarian reform throughout history or the French and Dutch refusal to follow the English path of enclosure and land concentration, something different from the two sets of initiatives that the conventional thinking of today imagines that government can take with respect to a market economy. They did not regulate the agricultural market. Nor did they diminish the inequalities of its outcomes through recourse to retrospective correction in the forms of progressive taxation and redistributive social spending. They innovated in the legally defined institutional arrangements of the market economy. They created a new kind of agricultural market. By so doing, they changed the primary distribution of economic advantage and powerfully contributed to the acceleration of economic growth on the demand as well as on the supply sides of the economy.

If we were to compare agricultural labor productivity in an economy (like the nineteenth-century English economy) that had undergone a dramatic concentration of land ownership and scale of production to one (like the nineteenth-century French economy) that had resisted it, we would find the former to be marginally higher than the latter. However, this measurement would fail to capture the benefit of a wide distribution of stakes in productive assets for economic growth through its effect on both supply and demand. It would even fail to do justice to the consequences of widely distributed ownership of land for labor productivity in other sectors of the economy; in the comparison of nineteenth-century Britain and France, lower French labor productivity in agriculture was compensated for by higher French labor productivity in manufacturing.

The institutional initiatives shaping the primary distribution of economic advantage need not themselves be economic in nature. They may have to do with access to educational opportunity or with sharing in political power. The central point remains the same. The institutional arrangements and ideological assumptions that organize how a society makes its future are the highest object of transformative ambition in politics. Everything that has to do with them and with their reconstruction is more important than anything that takes them for granted.

Among such arrangements and assumptions influencing the primary distribution of economic advantage and defining the terms of access to productive resources and opportunities, including the terms on which economic agents can cooperate in production and make use of other people's labor, one set of institutions deserves special attention. They are the arrangements that help spread the most advanced practice of production to parts of the economy other than those in which the practice first emerged. Alternatively, they are the initiatives that incorporate more workers and resources into the most productive part of the economy—in conformity to the chief recommendation of classical development economics.

When prescriptions like the message of twentieth-century development economics worked, they contributed to economic growth on both the supply and the demand sides of the economy. At the same time that they raised the average level of productivity in the economy, they created a class of relatively privileged workers whose wages could rise because the wage represented, in these most productive portions of the economy, a diminishing portion of the cost of production. The decline of mass production and the failure of the practical formula of development economics to continue working force us to put the simultaneous breaking of the constraints on the expansion of demand and of supply on a more reliable basis. That basis is inclusive vanguardism.

We now reach the fourth level of ways to break through the demand constraints on economic growth: the deepening and dissemination of the knowledge economy—the theme of this book. It is, in some respects, only a subset of the third level of initiatives: those reshaping the institutional arrangements that influence the primary distribution of economic advantage. However, this subset has special potential: first, because it promises to loosen or reverse the constraint of diminishing marginal returns to inputs in production; second, because it has perpetual rather than episodic innovation for an ideal; and third and most fundamentally, because of the combination of two features of an inclusive vanguardism that distinguish its potential relation to the whole economy from the place that all previous advanced practices of production have occupied in economic life.

The first feature is that unlike all earlier most advanced productive practices, it lacks an intrinsic relation to any one area of production. So long as it remains in the embrace of high-technology industry, it fails to reveal its deeper characteristics and to develop its greater potential. The second feature is that because, unlike mass production, it cannot be reduced to a small stock of formulaic machines, practices, and skills, it places heavy demands on the social, cultural, and political settings in which it takes hold.

My earlier argument about the cognitive-educational, social-moral, and legal-institutional requirements of inclusive vanguardism explores the content of these demands as moves in a pathway rather than as parts of a system. Each of these moves is more than just a means to the economy-wide spread of the most advanced practice of production. It has independent value as a contribution to the making of a higher cooperative regime. Such a regime does more than satisfy our interest in economic growth and its promise to liberate from poverty, infirmity, and drudgery. It also serves our stake in the enhancement of agency—the ability of each individual to rise above his circumstances and to share in the invention of the new.

The spectrum of breakthroughs in the constraints on supply

Consider now the hierarchy of ways of breaking through the supply-side constraints on economic growth. Once again, I go from the weakest and most short-lived to the strongest and most sustainable way to overcome these constraints. Each level has its own economic logic, characteristic practices, and distinctive limitations.

Hitting against these limitations never leads automatically to the next level: to move from one level to the next, there needs to be a reorientation of strategies, attitudes, and ideas. Until we near the top of the ladder, supply fails to ensure its own demand—not only in the special circumstances on which Keynes focused but across a broad range of economic conditions and historical moments. No move up a ring of this ladder guarantees a corresponding move up the ladder of ways of overcoming the demand constraints on economic growth. There is no correspondence between rungs of the ladder on one side and rungs on the other side, other than to observe a loose similarity of potency: the weak to the weak and the strong to the strong.

As we reach the end of this spectrum, however, the situation changes: what expands supply also expands demand; supply and demand adjust to each other in ways that drive economic growth by a rise in productivity, not simply by the accumulation of inputs. At the end of the spectrum we reencounter the development of a widespread knowledge economy: inclusive vanguardism.

To explore this set of ways of expanding supply, I adopt a heuristic device. I view the supply side from the standpoint of a representative or modal firm: a firm whose practices are most characteristic of the production system as a whole in a particular moment. It is true that at any given time, there will be firms that remain at the weak, early steps of these ways of pushing back the supply constraints of the economy and other firms that have risen further up the ladder. However, the economy is not just a collection of firms; to view it as such would be to commit a fallacy of composition. Except in moments of extreme disorientation and contradiction, certain practices, as well as the attitudes and ideas with which they are associated, prevail and give the economy a characteristic impulse. One of the most revealing features of this predominant behavior and consciousness of the agents of production is the extent to which their endeavors leave the economic institutions unchanged, untouched, and even unseen, or on the contrary press against the limits of these institutional arrangements.

At the first level, the representative firm produces only in response to manifest demand, minimizing inventory. It does not build inventory or expand output in anticipation of future demand. It does not seek to innovate in its practices or technologies. Such an orientation represents a hypothetical limiting case in which economic growth, if it is to occur, must be driven solely by demand.

At a second level, the firm builds up inventory in anticipation of future demand. It does so passively, however, without seeking to develop new markets and customers or to change its methods of production.

At a third level, the firm expands output without significant innovation in what and in how it produces, except to the extent that cost cutting may require rearrangement (e.g., doing the same with fewer workers and less capital). It goes in search of new customers and markets and seeks to strengthen its position against competitors in its established markets. Its primary concern is to increase the return on capital by minimizing competition and costs while increasing and defending market share.

At a fourth level, the firm innovates as well as expands. Its innovations aim to increase the efficiency and diminish the costs with which established goods and services are produced: they result in a better version of a familiar product, with a higher return on capital. Such innovations are efficiency-enhancing and capital-sparing. They do not revolutionize production; they progress by the accumulation of many small improvements.

At a fifth level, the firm practices what Christensen has called disruptive innovation: it combines new technologies and business models to produce a variant of an existing product at a much lower price, thus making it available to a broader mass of consumers, or to produce something new, for which it creates the market, finds the consumers, and arouses their desires. Such innovations are transformative: they create new assets in new ways and help make markets—and even wants—that did not exist before.

Here the modal firm operates on the demand as well as on the supply side of the economy. It does so, however, in a context in which economic institutions and policies have failed to ensure repeated and reciprocal breakthroughs of the demand and supply constraints on economic growth. In such an economic order, which is every existing or past example of a market economy, there is no institutional equivalent to Henry Ford's impossible contract: that he would pay his workers so well that they would be able to buy his cars.

Disruptive innovation represents in this sense an adaptation of the insurgent, opportunistic, and innovative firm to the lack of an economy-wide solution to the problem that this section addresses: the absence of a growth-promoting solution to the problem of the reciprocal adjustment of supply and demand. Contrary to the established way of thinking, no such solution results spontaneously from the workings of a variant of the present form of the market economy that has been expunged of failures of competition.

Reinterpreted along these lines, disruptive innovation is a way for the disruptive firm to profit at the micro level, in its own world, from the absence of the solution to the problem of the lack of upward growth and reciprocal adjustment between supply and demand at the macro level, in the economy as a whole. The firm creates its own demand, given that the economy will not do so for it. It is a micro approach to a macro problem: the disruptive innovators profit, but the deep sources of expansion of the economy on both the supply and the demand sides—the institutional arrangements of the economy, the way in which people are educated, and the organization of the state and of the contest over governmental power—lie beyond their reach and their concerns.

We cannot make up for this limitation by simply doing whatever we can to encourage the emergence and development of more such disruptive firms. For one thing, disruptive innovation by the firm is no guarantee of success; most who have attempted it have failed in their competition with nondisruptive businesses, those that remain content to pursue efficiency-enhancing, capital-sparing innovations. Disruptive innovation is not a practice that could take over the economy by the sheer force of competitive advantage.

More fundamentally, the task of broadening access to opportunities and capabilities on the supply side of the economy while elevating the returns to labor and the purchasing power of the broad mass of men and women is not one that can be executed through the application of any degree of entrepreneurial ingenuity. It requires structural change, set by the great forces of politics and thought, which shape the institutional presuppositions of the market outside the market.

Instead of just having more disruptive firms, we would have to have more disruptive people—individual practitioners of disruptive innovation. Such individuals would be formed by the conditions of an inclusive vanguardism: among them, the dialectical approach to education, the propagation of an experimentalist impulse in every department of social life, and the protection of vital protected stakes, safeguards, and endowments, making it possible for their beneficiaries to remain unafraid and capable in the midst of quickened change. To thrive, the disruptive individuals need an economic as well as a political order suitable to their dispositions. It cannot be one in which their impulses remain confined to an elite of upstart firms.

Here we reach the limits of the heuristic device provided by a representative firm. The view becomes that of the whole economy and of those who struggle in politics and thought to reshape the economic order.

The sixth level of breakthrough of the constraints on supply abandons the micro vantage point of the firm in exchange for the macro perspective of change in the economic arrangements and of their background in education and in politics. Once we view the problem from this encompassing standpoint, we risk being overwhelmed by its ambition and complexity. Where do we begin and with what instruments can we work? It may seem that every part of the task presupposes material, moral, and intellectual resources the lack of which is the condition of its importance.

The career of the defective and now impractical message of classical development economics—the boost to growth to be achieved by transferring workers and resources from less productive agriculture to more productive industry— contains a clue to the solution to this conundrum. The fixation on one sector of the economy—manufacturing— has ceased to be justified when the most advanced practice of production is present in every part of production and when the division of the economy into distinct sectors has lost its clarity.

What was most advanced then—industrial mass production—no longer is, and has ceased to ensure unconditional convergence to the frontier of growth in the world economy. It is now possible to develop mass production and to remain a relatively poor and backward economy, operating with cheap labor, and disconnected from the network of productive vanguards in the world, except as a supplier of the commoditized and subordinate pieces of production chains that are commanded by participants in that network—what I have called mass production as sidekick of the vanguard. Even in the historical reality that classical development economics addressed, the strategy of shifting people and resources into the most favored sector rather than disseminating the most advanced practice to every sector represented an adaptation to circumstance. In that circumstance, unlike in ours, the most advanced practice was more closely associated with one sector—manufacturing—than with all others.

Despite the limitations that have now made it all but unusable, the old message of development economics represents an incomplete expression of a powerful truth. The truth is that the best way to generate broad-based economic growth is to develop and disseminate throughout the economy the most advanced practice of production. Today that practice is no longer related to any particular sector; the proof that it is not is that it is present in every sector, if only as a fringe from which most workers and firms remain locked out.

The most promising way to overcome the supply-side constraints on the economy is to embrace the agenda of inclusive vanguardism. By understanding its conditions, we break it up into pieces and turn it into a program on which we can act. By acting on it, we raise the average productivity of the economy. We do so not through a one-time assimilation of new technologies (as happened in the United States in the period from 1994 to 2005) but through the generalization of a practice. This practice renders innovation habitual and increases its attractions and rewards by promising to lift the constraint of diminishing marginal returns to further commitments of the same input.

It may not seem obvious that the advances on the supply side of the economy that I explored in my earlier analysis of the conditions of inclusive vanguardism also work to break the constraints on the expansion of demand. Yet they do. To recognize how they do so, it is necessary to take into account another part of that analysis: a series of changes in the legal and institutional terms of access to the resources and opportunities of production and in the legal status of labor that must accompany the radicalization and dissemination of the knowledge economy.

These changes reshape the distribution of power within a market, between labor and capital, and between capital takers and capital providers: power to make decisions about the allocation of capital and the organization of work. Economic advantage, including a stronger hand in claiming a bigger share in returns to capital or labor, results directly from economic power. The sixth level of initiatives breaking through supply constraints on economic growth also breaks through the demand constraints because such initiatives form part of a reallocation of power in the economy, against the background of changes in education and in politics that reassign power in culture and in the state.

In any generalized form of the knowledge economy, the corporate form and the unified property right cease to be the nearly exclusive legal instruments for the decentralization of access to the means of production. The disaggregation of the property right—the creation of a wide range of fragmentary, conditional, or temporary stakes in pieces of the apparatus of production—allows different kinds of stakes and stakeholders in the same productive resources to coexist. It also makes it possible to combine, to a greater extent than present arrangements do, the decentralization of economic initiative and the aggregation of resources, the better to achieve scale. The corporate form, with its internalization of what would otherwise be contractual relations among distinct parties, becomes simply the extreme pole of a spectrum. At the opposite pole lies the arm's-length bilateral executory contract. In the broad middle ranges of the spectrum we find forms of collaboration sharing in the nature of both contract and the firm, with incomplete and ongoing relational contracts leaning to the contractual side of the spectrum and partnerships or joint ventures pointing to the business-organization side.

In such an economy, economically dependent wage labor ceases over time to be the predominant form of free work. The higher, purer forms of free labor—self-employment and cooperation—win primacy by steps. Their ascent gives practical force to a conception of the hierarchy of forms of free labor that was shared, up until the middle of the nineteenth century, by both liberals and socialists. It implements their ideal, however, by doing what they failed to accomplish: to reimagine the institutional form, and therefore the legal expression, of the market economy. The picture that emerges is that of an economy in which teams of worker-entrepreneurs, professionals, or technicians work together in a wide range of ways, almost all of which go beyond the arm's-length contract, oriented to a single, instantaneous performance, but most of which stop short of the corporate form.

Only such an institutional reshaping of the market order for the sake of a decentralization of access to productive resources and opportunities can make a deepened and widespread knowledge economy possible.

Take, by way of example, one of the characteristics of such an economy: its struggle to change the relation between the worker and the machine. Instead of mimicking the moves of his machine (as under mass production), the worker runs ahead of his technological equipment, even if it bests him, as artificial intelligence already has and increasingly will, in a wide range of powers. He reserves as much of his time as possible for that which cannot yet be done by machines because we have not yet learned how to render it formulaically. The ideal of the technical division of labor becomes the combination of the machine with the worker, as anti-machine.

It is an ideal that remains unlikely to be realized so long as the organization of production continues to rely on the corporation, the unified property right, and the primacy of economically dependent wage work among varieties of free labor. Under these conditions any change in the

224

relation between worker and machine will remain subordinate to the profit and power interests of owners and of those who rule the firm in their name. Change on the supply side can be achieved only by institutional and legal innovations that by shifting the balance of power between capital and labor influence the demand side.

From this example of a long-term, remote innovation, I turn to examples of short-term, proximate changes. Even the earliest steps in the institutional agenda of an inclusive knowledge economy have implications for both the supply and the demand sides of the economy. They reshape who has access and how to the resources and opportunities of production. Among such early steps are the orchestration of access to advanced practice and technology in favor of small and medium-sized firms and the identification and propagation of successful practice followed later by policies and institutions that organize decentralized, pluralistic, and experimental coordination between governments and emerging businesses (to the end of spreading the knowledge economy) as well as cooperative competition among firms. For each of these initiatives, there is an income and wealth effect shadowing the empowerment effect.

Similarly, the overcoming of economically dependent wage labor as the major species of free work may begin in the development of a legal regime that protects, organizes, and represents workers in precarious employment relationships. Such a regime would prevent the reorganization of production on the basis of global networks of contractual arrangements from resulting in radical economic insecurity imposed under the euphemistic banner of labor-market flexibility. By enhancing the power of labor vis-à-vis capital it helps prevent the consolidation of a dual labor market and imposes an upward tilt to the returns to labor, encouraging innovation in the service of productivity.

Thus, at each step of the way, in its early and intermediate development as well as in the achievement of its potential further into the future, a knowledge economy for the many breaks the constraints on the expansion of supply only by also breaking the constraints on the expansion of demand. An inclusive vanguardism accomplishes through cumulative change in the organization of the market order what the dominant ideas in economics claim to happen automatically, if only we cleanse the established market regime of restraints on competition. What those ideas treat as a natural and spontaneous phenomenon turns out to be the reward for far-reaching change in economic institutions and practices.

18.

Economics and the Knowledge Economy

The imperative of structural vision

To understand the knowledge economy and its alternative futures we need more and better ideas than we have. We need to do to the most advanced practice of production now what Smith and Marx, in their time, did to the most advanced practice of production then: to take it as a source of insight into the deepest and most general features of economic life and as a misunderstood prophecy.

The crucial feature of the needed ideas is that they provide us with a way of thinking about structural change in the economy, by which I mean change in the institutional arrangements of exchange and of production. The economy is both a regime of exchange and a regime of production. No understanding of economic life that focuses on one of these two faces of the economy to the exclusion of the other can hope to be adequate.

Both as a regime of exchange and as a regime of production, the economy exists as a distinctive set of institutions and practices. The institutional details matter. For many decades, a major premise of economic and social study as well as of ideological debate has been that there exists a very restricted stock of institutional options for the organization of an economy and that each of these options has a predetermined legal and institutional content. One of them is the market economy or capitalism. According to a weaker, diluted version of this thesis, there is a small number of versions of each such option or type, such as the versions discussed in the contemporary literature on "varieties of capitalism."

A working assumption of my argument about confined and inclusive vanguardism contradicts this view in both its stronger and its weaker forms. There is no such restricted repertoire of ways of organizing an economy. Nor is there a natural and necessary way to organize a market economy. There is no such thing as capitalism if by capitalism we mean one of such types, recurring in history under certain conditions and endowed with an inbuilt institutional and legal architecture and governed by immutable regularities, like the ones studied, as laws, symmetries, and constants of nature, by fundamental physics.

Institutional regimes have far-reaching consequences: they shape the routines of social life. They may be more or less resistant to challenge and transformation. They may be entrenched against change, or they may help organize and provoke their own remaking. Even when they are entrenched, however, they are not indivisible systems, operating according to regularities associated with their type. We cannot derive their constitutive arrangements, or understand how they work or how they can change, by inference from abstractions like capitalism or the market economy.

The road from an insular to an inclusive vanguardism passes through changes in the institutions defining the

market order and underlying the arrangements of production. Is economics, as it is now understood and practiced,
an adequate guide in the effort to travel this road?

This economics, the one that exercises world-wide influence from its base in the economics departments of the
leading American research universities, is not primarily
the study of the economy. It is mainly the study of a method
pioneered by the marginalist theoreticians (Walras, Jevons,
and Menger among others) at the end of the nineteenth
century. The study of the economy by some other method
is not recognized as economics. The application of the
method to subjects that have no direct relation to production and exchange is often treated as an exercise in
economics.

Marginalism was contested from the outset. Even in late
nineteenth-century Britain, contemporaries of the marginalists like Alfred Marshall and Francis Edgeworth proposed
rival theoretical approaches. In his *Mathematical Psychics*
(1881) and other writings, Edgeworth sought to develop
economics as a psychological and behavioral science in the
spirit of Bentham. In his *Principles of Economics* (1890),
Marshall argued for the transformation of economics into
a science of loosely connected, path-dependent causal
sequences, in the manner of natural history. These alternative approaches have resurfaced in less articulate and more
modest forms in the subsequent history of economics.
They have rarely challenged the ascendancy of the view
and method inaugurated by the marginalists.

Much of what economists do, working within the
marginalist tradition, has been, and increasingly is, pains-
taking empirical inquiry, seemingly free of commitment

to any restrictive theory. They pursue such inquiry through the formulation of models that seem compatible with a wide range of theories, including causal conjectures imported from other branches of social or psychological study.

This impression of intellectual capaciousness and elasticity is, however, an illusion. The main line of economics since the late nineteenth century has a distinctive direction, which the study of its limitations in what follows will make clear. These deficiencies disqualify it from furnishing some of the intellectual equipment that we need to think through the agenda of inclusive vanguardism.

The economics that descends from marginalism is a useful and even indispensable tool for thinking about the economy and its reshaping. It makes a decisive contribution to logical clarity, especially about trade-offs and constraints. In its role of presenting the bill to the dreamer, it resembles the slave who stood at the side of the *triumphator* in the Roman triumphal processions and whispered into his ear: remember that you will die. However, it cannot all by itself and without fundamental reconstruction and reorientation supply the ideas needed to inform answers to the most important issues in the economic life of contemporary societies: the antidotes to economic stagnation and inequality and the requirements of passage from insular to inclusive vanguardism.

It is common to defend the established practice of economic theory by protesting that there is no available better alternative—not at least one that combines a general approach to the economy with analytic practices that can be rigorously deployed. Even the most successful economic heresy of the last hundred years, Keynes's economics, has failed to be developed by its votaries into an alternative and equally comprehensive account of economic phenomena. Instead it has been cast (especially by its American followers) in the role of a mere complement to received theory. Represented as the theoretical basis for countercyclical management of the economy, Keynesianism has been reduced to a "macroeconomics" that is superimposed without tension on the received body of marginalist thinking, relabeled "microeconomics." In this already diminished role it has been attacked first as a reliable guide to economic policy and finally for any insight that could not, if valid, be translated back into the marginalist view. The lack of a successful alternative to the economics founded by the marginalists makes it all the more important to struggle to develop one.

To create the intellectual tools that we need, we must understand what the deficiencies of the main line of economic theory are. The most familiar criticisms of the established economics fail to provide this instruction: they are at best half-truths. They criticize economics for its simplifications as if simplification in the form of selectivity were not the condition of theorizing. They attack economics for using explanatory models that idealize the market order as if one of the aims of established analytic practice were not to explore the content and significance of the contrasts between the deliberate simplifications of its models and the workings of a real economy. They accuse economics of representing economic agents as calculating automatons as if the idea of maximization were not a vehicle for logical clarity and as if the deviation of economic behavior from the script of the maximizing automaton had not been for many decades a major concern of economists. To form another project in economics, we require another critique of the economics that we have inherited from the marginalists and their successors.

I describe the core of the marginalist conception of the economy. I go on to discuss the four central defects of the economics that resulted from the marginalist turn. The correction of these defects is the outline of a program for the reformation of economics and for its conversion into the discipline that we require to understand the confined form of the knowledge economy and to imagine its inclusive form. I then address the uses and limits of two sources of inspiration in this project: Keynes's contained heresy and pre-marginalist economics, especially as represented by the two greatest thinkers in the history of economic thought, Smith and Marx.

My argument about economics concludes by suggesting two ways to carry forward the intellectual agenda that I propose explicitly in this section and have anticipated, by implication, in the argument of this book. One route is the development and reconstruction of economics from within, taking its professional culture and methods as points of departure. The other route is from outside the established discipline and its procedures. This approach from the outside gathers its instruments from wherever it can find them; it understands economics as social theory applied to the phenomena of production and exchange.

We have no basis on which to affirm the superiority of either of these routes to the other one. We have every reason to try both and to see how far we can advance in the hope that further ahead they may converge.

This book travels the second path: the route from outside. It does not travel it in the form of a general study of economics, married to the explicit proposal of a way to think about economic problems. It travels it by addressing a particular topic—one that has immense consequence for the future of the economy and the society and special value as a prompt to reconsider our economic ideas: the nature and futures of the knowledge economy.

I now make explicit the requirements to develop the ideas of this book into a general way of thinking about the economy. And just as the program of inclusive vanguard-ism starts with what exists—the confined and superficial form of the knowledge economy—so this statement of the way of thinking can begin in the interpretation and criti-cism of the economics that we have inherited: the best organized and most influential of the social sciences.

The large-scale history of social and economic thought: truncating and evading structural vision

Before addressing the marginalist turn in the history of economics, it is useful to place that turn and its conse-quences in the context of the broader history of social theory and social study. To their disadvantage, economists have generally professed indifference to that history of ideas. It is all but impossible, however, to understand and to evaluate what has happened to their discipline without taking this intellectual-historical setting into account.

The central object of study in classical European social theory was the nature, genesis, and transformation of economic, political, and social regimes: the deep structure of institutional arrangements and ideological assumptions that shape the surface routines of society and organize the way in which economic capital, political power, and cultural authority are used to make the future within the present.

Karl Marx's theory of society and history was the consummate achievement of European social theory. At the core of this theoretical tradition lies a revolutionary insight: that the basic arrangements of a society are artifacts. We make them, in a daze of limited understanding and under the constraints of circumstances that we do not choose. It requires only a step beyond this conception to think of the institutional regimes or structures of society as a kind of frozen fighting: they are the arrangements and assumptions that remain to shape social life when our struggles over the terms of our relations to one another are interrupted or contained.

The idea of frozen fighting suggests that the sense in which the structures exist and are entrenched against challenge and change is variable, indeed one of the most important variables in history. The more such institutional and ideological regimes bar themselves against revision and acquire, as a result, the specious semblance of naturalness and necessity, the more powerful they become to determine the future as well as the present. They appear to us as an alien fate. They seem to deserve to be studied in the way we study the stars and the rocks. They rob us of a power that is ours, and that we would win back if we could reverse their recalcitrance to change.

We cannot disentrench them simply by affirming in theory their character as artifacts. We can do so only by reforming our institutions and practices so that they facilitate their own transformation and diminish the distance between the ordinary moves that we make within institutional and ideological frameworks that we take for granted and the extraordinary moves by which we challenge and change pieces of the framework. We know that we have succeeded when the extraordinary practice of changing a piece of the framework becomes ordinary, even banal, helping raise the experience and capabilities of ordinary men and women to a higher level of intensity and power.

The knowledge economy in its deepened and widespread form has a close affinity with this ideal, and exemplifies it in the prosaic activities of production. It does so both directly and indirectly: directly by adopting practices conducive to perpetual innovation and indirectly by virtue of its educational, moral, and institutional conditions.

The revolutionary insight into the made and imagined character of the social regime was compromised in classical social theory, and most clearly in Marxism, by a series of illusions, with decisive consequences for the subsequent development of social thought. The first illusion is the closed-list thesis: there is a closed list of alternative regimes of economic and political organization such as Marx's "modes of production." History runs through the list. Whatever powers of innovation we have with respect to its composition are severely limited. The second illusion is the indivisibility thesis: each of these regimes is an indivisible system, with an inbuilt institutional and legal content. It follows that politics must consist either in the revolutionary substitution of one such system for another or in the reformist management of one of these systems. The result is to exclude change that is structural in content and consequence but gradual or fragmentary in method. The third illusion is the laws-of-history thesis: higher-order regularities, which we are powerless to escape or reshape, rule the succession of these indivisible systems. There can be no major role for the programmatic imagination; history supplies for us the only program that counts.

The later evolution of social theory is the record of loss of faith in these beliefs. Historical learning and political experience alike have discredited them. The result, however, has not been the reaffirmation and radicalization of the central insight that those illusions circumscribed and even eviscerated. It has been the increasing dilution of the claims embodied in the illusions. Instead of generating out of the criticism of classical social theory—and of Marxism in particular—a theoretical view as ambitious as that of Marx, the successors to Marx's theory and to the tradition of classical social theory have watered down the original ideas while retaining its vocabulary. For example, they continue to speak of "capitalism" as a system, with its preset institutional and legal logic, and its fated passage through early and late stages, ending in foreordained crisis, although they may no longer believe in the assumptions that make sense of this usage.

Would an inclusive knowledge economy be a continuation of capitalism or a break with it? Its legal and institutional requirements, culminating, among many other changes, in the overcoming of economically dependent wage labor as the predominant form of free work and in a diversification of forms of decentralized access to the resources and opportunities of production, implies an economic regime incompatible with capitalism, as Marx and his followers understood it. Yet at no point would there be a sudden or wholesale shift from one system to another. Wage labor might cease to be predominant without disappearing. The unified property right would remain one of many vehicles of economic decentralization. The market order would no longer be fastened to a single version of itself. The question about whether the form of the knowledge economy explored in this book remains capitalism cannot be answered because the argument for inclusive vanguardism rests on social-theoretical premises incompatible with those underlying the concept of capitalism.

The social sciences that developed in the course of the twentieth century rejected the illusions only by also abandoning the central insight that they undermined: the crucial influence of an institutional and ideological framework that is left unchanged, unchallenged, and even unseen in the midst of our ordinary activities. The dominant impulse of these sciences has been to evade the task of understanding structural realities and of imagining structural alternatives.

Each of these sciences has denied in its own way the distinction, in every historical circumstance, between a deep framework of formative arrangements and assumptions and a surface life of routine activities and conflicts shaped by such a framework. Each has suppressed the imagination of structural discontinuity and alternatives. Each has naturalized the present stock of ways of organizing every part of social life. Each has represented the established arrangements as the outcome of an evolutionary convergence toward what works best or as the enduring residue of our ordinary practices of solving problems and accommodating interests. Each has helped cast a retrospective halo of naturalness, necessity, and authority on an improbable history.

Each social science has naturalized the organization of society, broken the link between insight into the actual and imagination of the adjacent possible, and evaded the work of structural understanding in its own way. The way taken by economics has been uniquely successful. As it was refounded by the marginalist theoreticians in the late nineteenth century, economics has overshadowed all other social sciences in its analytical accomplishments and its practical influence. It remains, despite all its limitations, the single most important source of the methods of thought, if not of the substantive conceptions, that we need to develop the program of inclusive vanguardism. In its present state, however, it is not enough. To supply what it fails to give us, we must reckon with its legacy.

Reckoning with post-marginalist economics: the disconnection between theory and empiricism

Walras, Jevons, Menger, and their allies and followers proposed to view the economy as a set of connected markets. Supply responds to demand, and demand to supply. Their reciprocal balancing forms the essence of the operation of a market. The medium through which supply and demand adjust to each other is the system of relative prices.

The explanation of relative prices became the hypothetical exercise around which marginalism developed. It was hypothetical because the analytic apparatus that the marginalists produced has never been used to explain actual relative prices in any real economy. Individual desires for consumption or gain drove supply and demand; hence the methodological individualism that marked, from the beginning, this approach to economics. The perspective was that of the individual making choices about the disposition of scarce resources that would most efficiently achieve his goals of consumption or gain.

This simple but immensely fertile way of thinking made it possible to chart economic life (understood as market-based exchange organized by relative prices) with great precision. Its radical simplifications allowed much of its analysis to take mathematical form. I call it here post-marginalist economics in the sense of the economics that arose from the marginalist turn and has remained in communion with its central line, rather than in the sense of an economics that proposed to move beyond marginalism.

Among the motivations of the marginalist reorientation, two deserve special emphasis. The first motivation was to overcome, by a single stroke, the confusions about value and price that had plagued preclassical economics, including the economics of Smith and Marx. The preclassical theory of value combined and confused the explanation of relative prices with the search for factors beyond supply and demand that accounted for the worth of assets—the ultimate sources of wealth. There resulted an endless series of conundrums, expressed, for example, in discussion of the relation between "exchange value" and "use value." It was a merit of the new economics to abandon the scholastic concept of value and provide a way of thinking, without reference to ultimate value, about relative prices.

A second, more important and less understood motivation of the marginalist turn was to create an economic science whose analytic power would be independent of positions taken in the causal and normative controversies that were so acute in the world at the time in which the marginalists came to intellectual maturity. The Austrian economists were right to understand this economics as a form of inquiry closer to logic than to causal science. Its defining move was to create an analytic apparatus, centered around competitive selection in connected markets, that generated explanations or conclusions only by being combined with factual stipulations, causal conjectures or theories, and normative commitments supplied to economics from outside itself. The more rigorously the analytic practice was deployed, the emptier it was of any such stipulations, conjectures, theories, and commitments. Its emptiness was the price of its vaunted neutrality and invulnerability. The fuel to make the analytic machine run could not come from inside the machine. In the history of social study over the last two centuries, there has never been a close counterpart to this intellectual strategy with the sole exception of Hans Kelsen's "pure theory of law."

The consequences of this approach were far-reaching and many-sided, although they are now concealed by the emphasis of contemporary economics on empirical research. These consequences can be summarized by the proposition that there is theory and empiricism in economics but that they have little to do with each other.

The quasi-logical schema lying at the center of this economics—maximizing choice under conditions of scarcity—does not amount to a theory. It makes no causal claims; it shapes a procedure of analysis that, when not abused, is as innocent of controversial causal claims as it is of contested normative commitments. It is a common misunderstanding of this procedure, one in which economists have often been complicit, to interpret it as a behavioral or psychological theory like the one that Edgeworth proposed at the time when Walras was writing or even like the less ambitious and more empirical work of contemporary behavioral or neuroeconomics.

Against the background of the quasi-logical conception of competitive selection and maximizing choice, under conditions of scarcity, explanation proceeds by building analytical models, susceptible to mathematical expression. If a model fails to describe or predict accurately the phenomenon, you make another one, by altering its elements or the values given to its parameters. (Another Marx said: "I have principles, and if you don't like them, I have other ones.") If the models have enough scope over a range of economic life or of economic change to support causal explanation, the required causal theories must be either fabricated ad hoc or imported from some other avowedly causal discipline, such as psychology. The proliferation of models does nothing to bring the underlying theory into question, provided that the theory is understood, in the marginalist spirit, austerely and rigorously enough.

The history of the main line of economic theory since the early marginalists has moved in two directions. The problem is not that these two directions contradict each other; it is that they do not. They coexist peacefully without engaging each other. One direction has been the progressive generalization of the quasi-logical view. Its culmination was the general-equilibrium analysis of the mid-twentieth century. The other direction has been empirical study.

The marriage of the analytic procedure of marginalism with empirical research is infertile. Causal theorizing must guide empirical study. No causal theory, or set of such theories, can be found in the early or late versions of this analytical approach. One of its leading ambitions was to carry no such theories within itself.

In a causal science, an accumulation of contrary facts eventually undermines a theory. Abstract and ambitious scientific theories, such as any of the reigning systems in the history of fundamental physics, can resist factual invalidation for a long time. The rearrangement of the relations among the central propositions of such a system, or the multiplication of context-bound qualifications, can accommodate inconvenient facts. Eventually, however, the dike breaks and the dominant theory is swept aside.

Such ruptures cannot happen in a sufficiently pure and rigorous version of this practice of economic analysis because the practice suppresses or avoids the dialectic between theoretical inquiry and empirical investigation. One model can give way to another without causing trouble for the underlying theoretical account of the economy. This account was always closer to logic than to causality and science—and therefore to mathematics as a tool of logical clarity rather than to mathematics as an instrument of surprising causal discovery.

Rather than being an advantage, as the marginalist theoreticians and their successors have supposed, the immunity of the underlying theory to attack is a liability. It condemns the would-be science to an eternal infancy. The economics that we need the better to think through the program of inclusive vanguardism must make falsifiable causal claims based on controversial causal theories. Its models and its mathematics must remain subordinate to its explanatory ambitions.

Reckoning with post-marginalist economics: the deficit of institutional imagination

A second defect of the economics that the marginalists created is its poverty of institutional imagination. The most important form of this poverty regards the assumptions that this economics makes about the institutional and legal form of the market economy. When it is not, at its most rigorous, silent about the institutional form of the market, it falsely equates the idea of the market with a particular, historically contingent set of market arrangements that developed, and came to prevail, in the economies with which it deals.

We can distinguish three types of post-marginalist economics by the criterion of how they deal with the institutional definition of the market order. Call the first type pure economics. It is agnostic about the institutional form of the market and pays a price for this agnosticism in the reach of what it can say and propose. The second and third types—fundamentalist and equivocating economics—are alternative versions of the unwarranted identification of the market idea with the private law and the economic arrangements that evolved in the history of the North Atlantic countries: the second explicitly and aggressively, the third without conviction or constancy. The major lesson of this story is simple. The economics created by marginalism is either pure and impotent (in its ability to explain as well as to propose), or it is potent and compromised (by its unjustified identification of the idea of a market with a particular institutional version of the market economy).

Pure economics, as espoused by the early marginalists and by their most uncompromising successors, avoids all commitment to institutional assumptions. The procedure of competitive selection under conditions of scarcity may not even need to be embodied in any decentralized or market economy; it may be mimicked, according to the outcome of a mid-twentieth-century debate, by an economy under central direction. Pure economics is as indifferent to the imagination of alternative versions of the market economy as it is to the identification of maximizing rationality with a particular set of institutional arrangements. By this austerity, it avoids the mistakes of the two types of economics that I next describe. By the same token, however, it deprives itself of the means with which to explain established economic institutions or to explore alternatives to them. The price of its austerity is its explanatory and programmatic impotence.

Fundamentalist economics equates the abstract idea of the market with a particular institutional system, expressed most fully by private law and, within private law, by the nineteenth-century law of property and contract, centered on the unified property right and the bilateral executory contract. Its clearest theoretical formulation is the view most comprehensively developed in the mid-twentieth century by Hayek: spontaneous exchange among free and equal agents automatically generates the same market order. We have only to prevent this natural recurrence to the intrinsic structure of spontaneous coordination from being interrupted or distorted by governmental meddling in the practice of competitive, market-based exchange. The same belief survives, with much less clarity but formidable tenacity, in the conviction of the practical economist that a market is a market, contract is contract, and property is property.

A hundred and fifty years of legal analysis have shown the opposite to be true. From the middle of the nineteenth century to the end of the twentieth, jurists discovered, often against their intentions and expectations, the legal and institutional indeterminacy of the market idea. They found that at every turn in the translation of general ideas about contract, property, and other aspects of the regime of market exchange into detailed rules, standards, doctrines, and practices there are choices to made: alternative ways to go down the ladder of concreteness. Such alternatives shape the arrangements of production and exchange as well as the distribution of economic advantage; they have to do with the constitution of the market economy, not simply with its distributive consequences.

The choices among the alternative routes to the detailed legal organization of a decentralized economic order turn on conflicts among interests and among visions as well as among clashing assumptions and conjectures about the consequences of each direction of change. We cannot settle such disputes by inferring their resolution from the abstract idea of the market or even from the next higher rung in the ladder of institutional and legal detail.

The fundamentalist thesis has striking implications: it excludes any attempt to reimagine and reshape the institutional framework of production. Just such a reimagination and such a reshaping are essential to the spread and deepening of the knowledge economy. In fact, they prove indispensable to any significant change in the character of production and of its most advanced practice; economic and technological forces operate in a formative institutional context.

The fundamentalist thesis continues to exert influence in watered down as well as in undiluted forms. An example of its dilution is the view that there exists a set of universally applicable practical principles of economic policy and organization. Such principles occupy a level of thought intermediate between pure economic theory and detailed institutional design. They are supported by the former and compatible with a wide range of forms of the latter. The aim is to combat the fundamentalist defense of a unique institutional program (as in the doctrine of institutional convergence to a set of best practices and institutions—those prized in the rich North Atlantic countries). But the goal is also to show the practical value of post-marginalist economics to the design of institutions.

We do not escape the flaws of the fundamentalist view by weakening it. The pure methods and ideas of the economics created by marginalism can generate no practical guides to institutional reconstruction whatsoever unless we combine them with factual stipulations, causal theories, and normative commitments external to pure economic analysis. And the principles claimed to enjoy universal applicability possess no such privilege. Consider some candidates for the role.

Respect the rights of property and the security of transaction to ensure investors of a return to their investments. But any structural change may upset vested rights. The rights of market incumbents conflict with the needs of new entrants. And property is simply a name for the detailed organization of access to the capital stock of society and to the resources and opportunities of production.

Keep money sound: do not generate liquidity beyond the increase in nominal money demand at reasonable inflation. But given the present circumstantial separation of powers among governments, banks, and central banks, the management of the money supply obeys multiple goals (as applicable American legislation explicitly recognizes). The central bank may manage money countercyclically, expanding the money supply in slumps and diminishing it in booms. Or the desire of a government to have a shield against the interests and preconceptions of the capital markets, the better to initiate a rebellious strategy of national development, may trump the reasons motivating such countercyclical policy.

The state may have reason to practice fiscal austerity— so as not to depend on financial confidence rather than to placate it. We cannot derive a position in such controversies about money from any general principle inherent in post-marginalist economic theory. We can generate it only from the combination of a political-economic program with a set of conjectures and theories about the likely effects of different policies and arrangements in a particular situation.

Target redistributive entitlements as closely as possible to their needy and intended beneficiaries. But the experience of European social democrats and American progressives in power has suggested the opposite: to withstand the pressure of downward movements in political-business cycles, a redistributive agenda must benefit ordinary working families rather than an insular group of the very poor. Nothing in pure economic analysis, in the mode of post-marginalist economics, recommends the targeting approach, only a set of commonsensical prejudices. Practical experience discredits them.

The attempt to find a stable middle position between the institutionally empty propositions of economic theory and the commitment to a particular set of institutional arrangements, in the form of supposedly universal principles of institutional design, fails. The propositions generate no institutional consequences. The supposedly universal guidelines are no more than rules of thumb informed by limited historical experience and motivated by contested political goals. Significant institutional innovations, like the innovations needed for the advancement of an inclusive knowledge economy, are likely to require defiance of such rules of thumb; one age's common sense is just the controversial philosophy of an earlier or a later age.

Equivocating economics seeks to establish regularities of economic life against an institutional background that it may recognize in principle to be decisive but that it disregards in its analytic and programmatic practice. Its habitual domain of application has been macroeconomics. The equivocating economist sets out to establish law-like regularities between large-scale economic aggregates, such as the levels of employment and inflation. An example is the idea of the Phillips curve, according to which there is a stable, quantifiable relation between the level of employment and the rate of inflation. If monetary and other policies push unemployment below its "natural rate," inflation will result. The regularities may appear to laws. By discovering them, economics would turn into the causal science that pure economics would not be and that fundamentalist economics cannot be.

Equivocating economics ordinarily studies such regularities without regard to their institutional assumptions, which it takes to be stable or constant. A critic of its work may object that such regularities—for example, those of the Phillips curve charting a supposedly law-like relation between unemployment and inflation—depend on a wide range of detailed institutional arrangements. It suffices to change any element of this background to alter the supposed regularities. For the Phillips curve, the formative institutional arrangements may include, for example, those that have to do with the labor-law regime and the type of union organization that it sustains, the nature and level of unemployment insurance, and the assignment and scope of the power to set monetary policy. To play a role in such explanations, the institutional regime of economic life must be defined with the detail that remains missing from abstractions like capitalism or the market economy. Because the details change, and are the object of persistent controversy and conflict, we will find it hard to mistake such formative structures for indivisible systems or for recurrent types of social and economic organization.

The equivocating economist may concede that any change in the institutional background may undermine the regularities that he claims to have found, robbing them of their law-like character. If, however, this background is in fact relatively stable—as it has been in the North Atlantic countries of today—he will disregard this concession in his analytic and explanatory work. He will continue to do equivocating economics.

A practice of economic analysis that can overcome the deficiencies of pure, fundamentalist, and equivocating economics needs to change how economic theory approaches the relation between day-to-day economic activity and economic institutions. Its focus should become the relation of the phenomena of production and exchange to the institutional and ideological context—the structure—within which they occur and therefore as well the way in which this structure is imagined and made, and then reimagined and remade. Pure, fundamentalist, and equivocating economics cannot meet this test; they offer three ways of evading the imperative of structural insight.

Reckoning with post-marginalist economics: the theory
of production subordinated to the theory of exchange

A third limitation of the economics inaugurated by the
marginalist turn is its lack of any proper theory of production. It is a theory of competitive market exchange bereft
of any theory of production. Its view of production is a
straightforward extension of its theory of exchange, as
anyone can see by simply turning to the chapter on production in introductory economics textbooks. Even the
subfield of industrial organization takes as its primary
subject matter the shape of markets in different sectors of
the economy. Practical attitudes and experiences, encour-
aged by this limitation, in turn reinforce it. The economist
is more likely to be interested in hedge funds than in
factories.

Ever since the late nineteenth century, the main line of
economic thinking has viewed production through the
lens of exchange and of relative prices. This subordination
of the perspective of production to the perspective of
exchange was made easier by a particular feature of the
economies with which the new economics dealt: that in
them labor, which stands at the center of the realities of
production, can be bought and sold. When wage labor
becomes the overwhelmingly predominant form of free
work, the way is open to see the arrangements of production as simply one more terrain for the operation of relative prices.

Pre-marginalist economics, especially in the writings of
Adam Smith and Karl Marx, proposed an account of
production and of its historical transformation. This

account was not reducible to the theory of exchange. It occupied in the ideas of these economists a place at least as important as their ideas about markets, prices, and competition. Smith and Marx studied factories: the workshops of the then most advanced practice of production—mechanized manufacturing—ranked among the chief inspirations of their thinking.

In this book, concerned as it is with the nature and future of the now most advanced productive practice, the knowledge economy, the most pertinent part of economics is the study of production. It falls to this study to show what the most advanced practice of production reveals about basic and general features of economic life, such as the relation between the worker and the machine as it is and can become, and the relation between our experiments in the transformation of nature, supported by science and embodied in technology, and our experiments in the way we cooperate. These themes have decisive importance to the understanding of production and of its evolution. We cannot hope to master them as mere examples of market-based exchange. They do not disclose their secrets in the register of relative prices. Nor do they lend themselves to mathematical representation—not at least of the relatively simple kind that has served post-marginalist economics.

Every major element of the missing theory of production must be present in an argument about the nature and alternative futures of the most advanced productive practice.

Reckoning with post-marginalist economics: a
theory of competitive selection unaccompanied
by an account of the diversity of the material
from which competitive selection selects

A fourth deficiency of the economics inaugurated by the
marginalists is that as a theory of competitive market
selection it lacks an account of the creation of the diverse
stuff from which the selective mechanism selects. The
diversity available for selection is treated as external to the
concerns of economics. Post-marginalist economics
simply takes its range and richness and its very existence
for granted. It is an onerous failing: the fecundity of a
method of competitive selection depends on the variety of
the material with which it works.

Paul Samuelson described the Ricardian doctrine of
comparative advantage as the single most powerful insight
of economics. It is all the more powerful for being coun-
terintuitive. As does the whole of trade theory, it presupposes the division of the world into different economies
operating under the shield of sovereign states. The division
of the world in turn makes possible the adoption of distinct
institutional arrangements and supports the distinct ways
of being human that are the cultures of mankind. Different
economic institutions favor diversity in the development
of our productive capabilities: in what we produce and in
how we produce.

From the standpoint of the main line of economic theory
since the late nineteenth century, however, the division of
the world into economies separated by national frontiers
and governed by different laws is an accident without

economic significance, if it is not a costly embarrassment. There might just as well be a unified world economy under the aegis of a world government and its laws, free of the transaction costs and of the complications and risks, including armed conflicts as well as trade wars and real wars, that result from state sovereignty.

It is as if the neo-Darwinian synthesis in evolutionary theory were reduced to half of its present composition: the half about Darwinian natural selection unaccompanied by the other half about genetic mutation and recombination. The fecundity of a mechanism of competitive selection depends on both the effectiveness of the mechanism and the diversity of the material selected. To possess half of such an account without the other is to be left with a view of uncertain value: the value of the available half depends on its relation to the other, missing half.

The failure to develop an account of the diversification of the material from which competitive selection selects is closely related both to the absence of a view of production (other than as a shadowy extension of exchange) and to the deficit of institutional imagination (especially with respect to the possible arrangements of the market order). There may be greater or lesser experimental divergence in what is produced and in how it is produced. The institutions defining the market economy may favor or discourage the creation of new assets in new ways. They may tighten or loosen the link between our experiments with nature and our experiments in cooperation.

The creation of diversity is not a constant or a given; it is a task. The most important principle commanding the implementation of this task is that one kind of diversity help generate another. The best market order is the one that is not fastened to a single version of itself and that allows different legal regimes of decentralized access to the resources and opportunities of production (which is to say, different property regimes) to coexist in the same economy. The achievement of this result does not exempt us from the work of institutional design—the design of a regime accommodating multiple sets of arrangements for decentralized access to the resources and opportunities of production; it makes that work harder.

These remarks apply with special force to any economic theory that would elucidate the nature and future of the knowledge economy. The affinity of the present most advanced practice of production to a political economy giving a major role to the diversification of the material from which competitive selection selects is manifest in every aspect of the spread and deepening of the knowledge economy. Consider the matter at the two extremes of a spectrum that goes from the micro features of production engineering to its macro setting—the institutional framework of economic activity.

Even in its limited, insular form, the knowledge-intensive practice of production combines the destandardization or customization of goods and services with their making at large scale. At the same time, by raising the level of discretion and trust allowed and demanded of participants in the process of production it increases the room for experimental innovation and diversity in process as well as in products.

The deepening and dissemination of the knowledge economy require a wide range of arrangements for the organization and funding of decentralized economic activity, and therefore a plurality of regimes of property and contract. The defense and sharpening of market competition must have as its complement a widening of experimental diversity in the methods and outcome of economic activity. Instead of being assumed, the diversity must be sought and achieved by the institutions of the economy as well as by the practices of production.

An economics useful to such an agenda must be one that supplies the missing counterpart to a theory of competitive selection: the part about the stuff available for selection.

Uses and limits of Keynes's heresy

One of the resources at our disposal as we contend with the limitations of post-marginalist theory is the most striking and influential economic heresy of the twentieth century: Keynes's economics. Among its greatest strengths are its emphasis on the importance of money and of attitudes to the use of money balances, its introduction of the idea that supply and demand can come into balance at many different levels of economic activity, including at levels that leave activity lastingly depressed, and its consequent justification of governmental action to prevent society from having to pay a terrible cost for the insufficiency of the self-restorative powers of the market.

As a guide, however, to the economics that we need to think through the program of an inclusive knowledge economy and to make up for the limitations of economics after marginalism, Keynes's economics suffers from four connected defects.

Unlike Walrasian economics, Keynes's economics is not, at its most general and most rigorous, a quasi-logical inquiry. It does make causal conjectures on the basis of a partly explicit causal theory. However, it departs from the formalism of the marginalists and their successors only by exaggerating the emphasis of English political economy on psychology, to the detriment of institutions and structure. All the major categories of Keynes's theoretical system—the preference for liquidity, the propensity to consume, and the state of long-term expectations—are psychological rather than institutional or structural. Remember that all assume an unchanged institutional and legal framework of the market economy, except insofar as governmental activism in fiscal and monetary policy implies a reassignment of powers between private economic agents and the state. Institutional discussion in Keynes is almost entirely confined to particular corners of economic life (notably the stock market) and presented as ancillary to a larger view in which the great forces of fear, greed, illusion, and "animal spirits" play the leading part. It is futile to deal with the present and alternative futures of the knowledge economy without addressing the institutional organization and reorganization of the market regime.

A second failing of Keynes's economics as a source of the ideas we require is closely related to the first defect. Keynes dealt with the economy and with economic recovery primarily from the demand side, not from the supply side. But the transformation of production and of the role played by the most advanced productive practice in the economy calls for institutional thinking and imagination.

A Keynesian may object that Keynes's immediate concern was to rethink economics with a view to the great slump that he and his contemporaries confronted in the 1930s rather than to explain or to propose a change in the process of production. However, no slump can be understood, and no recovery organized, without attention to both the demand and the supply sides of the economy. The occurrence of successive breakthroughs of the constraints on supply and on demand is the fundamental requirement for sustained economic growth.

The failure of a breakthrough on the supply side to ensure a corresponding breakthrough on the demand side, or vice versa, is the chief source of economic instability, interrupting growth. (The secondary source of economic instability is the variable and dangerous relation of finance to the real economy.) Inclusive vanguardism is among other things a practical response to what might otherwise seem to be a merely theoretical enigma: it breaks through growth-limiting constraints on the demand as well as the supply sides of the economy. It reshapes the primary distribution of economic advantage instead of seeking merely to correct it retrospectively by progressive taxation and redistributive social entitlements and transfers.

This second limitation of Keynes's system in turn leads to a third flaw: as an account of economic breakdowns it is, as I earlier argued, the theory of a special case rather than a general theory of the ways in which supply and demand may fail to balance at full employment and with continued economic growth. It addresses a special case distinguished by inadequate demand, by the diversion of saving into unproductive hoarding, and by the downward rigidity of a particular price, the price of labor. To be a truly general theory of the failure of supply and demand to carry each other to the next level of incitement to economic growth, it would need to include a view of production and of its reshaping.

This failing explains why Keynesianism has been judged even by many of its followers to be an inappropriate or at least insufficient response to the "balance-sheet recessions" of the early twenty-first century. These recessions were prompted in part by the inability of debt, credit, and easy money, in the context of worldwide capital and trade imbalances, to make up for the lack of sustained rises in productivity and of broad-based, socially inclusive economic growth. It is also the reason why Keynes's doctrine has proved sterile as the basis for a response to the contemporary discourse on secular stagnation. The thesis of secular stagnation attempts to give a semblance of naturalness and necessity to economic slowdown in contemporary societies. It does so by attributing stagnation to causes beyond our control, such as the supposedly smaller potential of contemporary technologies when compared to the technological innovations of a hundred years ago.

The fourth deficiency follows from the third, as the third from the second and the second from the first. Keynes's economics is caught between being an account of a particular disequilibrium at a low level of activity and employment (the theory of a special case) and being a theory of persistent imbalance in the economy. Much in its spirit and its arguments undermines faith in the self-restorative powers of an idealized and reified market order—a market without a state, except insofar as a state is needed to protect the market and to administer its impersonal and unchanging laws—anytime and anywhere. To turn into a theory of permanent disequilibrium it would have needed to become the general theory of slumps that it is not. To become such a theory, it would have had to deal with the supply as well as the demand sides of the economy and with the institutional structure and possibilities of the established market order as well as with the impulses and illusions of economic agents.

These limitations of Keynes's heresy keep it from being the alternative to post-marginalist economics that we require. They also help explain the course that the main line of economics followed in the twentieth century.

The American followers of Keynes reduced his doctrine to a theory justifying countercyclical management of the economy by means of fiscal and monetary policy. They turned it into the intellectual and policy equipment of a mid-twentieth-century mixed, regulated economy. To this end, they redefined it as a macroeconomics: a specialized set of ideas orienting the relation of the state to the economy rather than a general alternative to the economics created by the marginalists. They then superimposed it on the untransformed but ever more generalized body of post-marginalist economic theory, redubbed microeconomics. They could not have accomplished this domestication of Keynes's doctrine unless it lent itself, by virtue of the deficiencies that I have described, to this diminishment.

Once Keynes's teaching had been deprived of any claim to serve as the point of departure for an alternative to the economics inaugurated by the marginalists and had been cast instead in the role of complement to it, the empire (the main line of economic theory) could strike back against its shrunken opponent. In the closing decades of the twentieth century, a series of rightwing proposals in practical economics, advanced under labels such as "rational expectations" and "real business cycle theory" attacked the superstructure of Keynesian macroeconomics as mistaken or dispensable, and argued that whatever was new in this theory (that is to say, not implied in the standard body of economic analysis) was false. Writing done under the label of the "micro foundations of macroeconomics" completed the work of destruction by reinterpreting Keynesian claims in ways that allowed them to be assimilated to the dominant ideas. This brief narrative summarizes all too much of the history of economics in the late twentieth and early twenty-first centuries.

That it reveals something deep about the path of the North Atlantic societies, as well as about the direction of economic theory, is shown by its close resemblance to what happened at the same time in the history of law and legal theory. The dominant practical concern of twentieth-century legal reform, and of the jurisprudence that supported it, was to share in the design of the social democratic settlement. The opponents of the established arrangements of power and production would abandon their challenge. In return, the state would be allowed to acquire the power to regulate the market more pervasively. It would be empowered to attenuate, through retrospective and compensatory tax-and-transfer, inequalities generated by the existing market regime. And it would be authorized to manage the economy countercyclically through fiscal and monetary policy without attempting to affirm significant governmental or public influence over the investment decision.

A new body of public law, the law of a regulatory and redistributive state, would be superimposed on a largely untransformed corpus of private law: the rules of property and contract, the constitutive arrangements of the market economy. Later, in the final decades of the twentieth century, this superstructure of public law and policy would begin to be attacked and circumscribed in the name of flexibility, efficiency, and even freedom. The fundamental weakness was the same as in practical Keynesianism: failure to reimagine and remake the arrangements of private law and of the market economy rather than just to place them in a new public-law setting.

Such an economic or legal theory can be of little use in guiding the formulation and advancement of a program of inclusive vanguardism. The task requires intellectual help that economic and legal theory in their present form fail to provide.

Uses and limits of the example provided by pre-marginalist economics

Another source of inspiration in the effort to deal with the limitations of the economics created by the marginalists is the economics that preceded marginalism, sometimes called classical economics. There are two species of classical economics, distinct in the scope of their subject matter and the range of their ambitions: the specialized science of political economy practiced by economists like Senior, Ricardo, Malthus, and Say, and the view of political economy as comprehensive social theory applied to the phenomena of production and exchange that Adam Smith and Karl Marx exemplified. My comments here about the uses and limitations of pre-marginalist economics take this second, more ambitious version of classical economics as their focus.

Smith and Marx differed radically in their intentions, methods, and ideas. They nevertheless resembled each other in what distinguished them from the economics that the marginalists created. We have no reason to emulate their example even if we could: the flaws of classical economics make it unusable as a ready-made alternative to the economics that resulted from the marginalist turn. Nevertheless, criticism of classical economics helps show the way to the economics that we need and lack.

Classical economics was free from at least three of the four defects of the economics inaugurated by the marginalists. It proposed causal theories and explanations. It was no quasi-logical inquiry, seeking immunity to causal controversy and resting its authority on logical clarity and rigor. It was not content to import its causal ideas from other disciplines or to make them up on the spot. It offered an account not just of the causal workings of the economy but also of the long-term evolution of economic life. Its core concern was the relation between institutional regimes and practices of production. It saw in the study of the most advanced practice of production a gateway to understanding the deepest and most general features of economic life. It viewed economic history as the history of institutional regimes. Each of these regimes imposed distinct constraints on the development of our powers and came with a distinct set of economic regularities. The history of the most advanced practices of production was also a history of institutional systems.

The economics that Smith and Marx practiced had institutional imagination. Its structural approach (to economic regimes and their making) was marred by the necessitarian illusions characteristic of the central tradition of European social theory: the belief in a short list of alternative regimes, in the indivisibility of each of them, and in their foreordained succession. For them, economics begins and ends in the understanding of a distinctive regime of economic life, with its assumptions, regularities, and consequences, and in the specification of the large forces— laws of historical change—that lead from one regime to another. The focus on structural discontinuity and progress was not disinterested: it served a magnanimous vision of unrealized human opportunity. Its impulse was prophetic as well as explanatory.

For Smith and Marx, economics was at least as much a theory of production as it was a theory of exchange. They did not treat the economy as if it were a trading house or a bank any more than they saw it as a large factory. They viewed productive activity as presenting economics with a series of problems that were irreducible to the operation of supply and demand in a market and that involved the relation between how we cooperate and how we mobilize and change nature for our benefit.

The economics of Smith and Marx was free (albeit at a cost) from what I have described as the first three defects of post-marginalist thinking—its disassociation of formal analysis and causal inquiry, its poverty of institutional imagination, and its sacrifice of the study of production to the study of exchange. However, it failed to escape the fourth deficiency of the economics invented by the marginalists: it lacked an account of the making of the diverse material from which the mechanisms of competitive market-based selection select.

Classical economics, in the grand version that it took at the hands of Smith and Marx, suffered from three defects (in addition to its failure to provide an account of diversification) that compromise its use today as an alternative to post-marginalist practice. I list them in the inverse order of their significance. The third flaw is decisive. Its correction requires an economics very different from the economic theories of Smith and Marx.

The first deficiency of pre-marginalist economics was its devotion to a lost cause in economic analysis: the formulation of a theory of value. Value theory served a dual purpose: to explain relative prices and to identify the ultimate source of the aggregation of value in economic life. It claimed to build a bridge between the surface (the system of relative prices) and the depth of economic life (the wellsprings of the creation of wealth). No such bridge could ever be built. The quasi-metaphysical conception of a substrate of value never had a precise, quantifiable meaning. The marginalists showed that a mathematical representation of supply and demand could in principle account for relative prices without any need to refer to underlying value. The confusion induced by the attempt to explain, on the same basis, relative value and the aggregation of value was reproduced within value theory itself in scholastic disputes about the relation between two imaginary entities: use value and exchange value. Although its equivocations about price and value were the least important of the defects of classical economics, it was the defect the resolution of which provided the immediate incitement to the marginalist turn. In this endeavor, the marginalists were unequivocally successful.

The second failing of classical economics, at the hands of its two major exponents, was its overstatement of the role of coercion in the economy and its corresponding understatement of the place of the imagination. The marriage of functionalist explanation (the consequences of a system are the cause of its existence) with the view of structure and structural change typical of classical European social theory set the stage for this exaggeration. For Marx, the basic explanation for the class character of society, and thus at a particular stage in the evolution of humanity for capitalism, was the need to ensure the coercive extraction of a surplus over current consumption. For Smith, the brutalization of humanity in the technical division of labor was the inescapable price of a quantum leap in productivity.

They were mistaken. It was not by virtue of having a higher rate of aggregate saving that late eighteenth-century Britain, followed by the United States and Western Europe, became the terrain of the Industrial Revolution.

Historical research has shown that aggregate saving in these economies was lower, not higher, than in many countries of the time that witnessed no such advance. The Western advantage lay in a series of technological, organizational, institutional, and conceptual innovations against the background of certain social, political, and cultural openings that made space for these innovations. It lay as well in the projection of military force, both to defend and to attack.

The technologies of mechanized manufacturing make it possible to organize work so that the worker acted as if he were his machine, endlessly repeating the same specialized movements. This reduction of labor to machine-like activity may have the advantage of facilitating the spread of this model of production by minimizing its educational requirements. But simple machines can also be deployed by people with complex capabilities to do whatever these people have learned how to routinize and save their time for other activities. The brutalization on which Smith remarked in the pin factory can be explained only by the co-evolution of the technology, the human resources, and the institutional and legal regime of this style of production with its reliance on managerial control exercised in the name of property.

As they exaggerated the need for coercion in the economies that they studied, Smith and Marx understated the role of innovation and of our imaginative powers. To the extent that it is disseminated and deepened, the knowledge economy places the imagination at the center of economic life. It calls for an economic theory for which the most advanced practice of production is the one that best reshapes cooperation on the model of imagination in all the ways that my argument has explored. But innovation and imagination were always more important to the economy than the coercive extraction of a surplus or the despotic direction of labor, except in the most primitive conditions of accumulation. The economics that we need must be one that recognizes their centrality.

The third and most important failing of classical economics, in its most ambitious version, is its taint by a flawed understanding of economic regimes: "commercial society" and its predecessors for Smith; "capitalism" and the other modes of production for Marx. It is the same view of structure as system that much of classical European social theory embraced in the nineteenth and early twentieth centuries. Smith, writing early in the history of this tradition of social theory, presented this conception loosely. Marx, the author of its most powerful expression, gave it its most systematic and comprehensive form. Both thinkers took the regime—its workings, character, and consequences—to be the chief subject matter of their economic theory.

They represented commercial society or capitalism as a recurrent type of economic organization and as a well-defined stage in our history. It had, for Marx much more than for Smith, an intrinsic institutional and legal content. They described this type as an indivisible system. We can manage it or replace it by another system if the constraints and regularities of history allow for such a substitution. However, we cannot reimagine and remake it step by step and piece by piece. For them, the most important task of economics was to explain the succession of economic regimes in history. It was also to account for the law-like workings of the regime that immediately concerned them—commercial society or capitalism—and the most advanced practice of production—mechanized manufacturing—that it supported.

They mistook, in these ways, the basic character of the economic regimes with which they dealt. The institutional and ideological framework of an economy exercises immense influence. It shapes the routines of both exchange and production. It is not, however, a natural phenomenon like the atomic structure of a piece of nature. Even the sense in which it exists is variable: the force with which it exists depends on the extent to which the institutional arrangements and discursive practices of the regime are organized to resist or to invite revision.

No regime forms an indivisible system, constituted on a take-it-or-leave-it basis. Institutional and ideological orders are ramshackle constructions: the outcomes of many loosely connected sequences of conflict among interests and among ideas. They change, we change them, step by step and part by part. Fragmentary, piecemeal, and discontinuous change is not only compatible with the transformation of such structures; it is close to being the only way in which they change.

They change under constraint but not according to a script governed by historical laws. Different regimes compete as possible settings for what Marx called the development of the forces of production. But the same functional advantage—of economic or military power—can always have alternative institutional foundations. An institutional innovation accepted for the sake of its practical rewards is often implemented only in the form that least disturbs dominant interests and prevailing preconceptions: what we might call the path of least resistance. The insular vanguardism that is the present form of the knowledge economy—the confinement of the most advanced practice of production to exclusive fringes in every sector of the economy—represents such a path of least resistance in our time.

The enemies of the path of least resistance are thought and democracy: thought about structures and their transformation, free from the illusions that undermined, in classical European social theory, our insight into the made and imagined character of social life; democracy, reshaped to master the established structure, without requiring crisis to serve as the condition of change.

Two ways to develop the needed ideas: from within the established economics and from outside it

A practice of economic analysis and argument useful in formulating the program of an inclusive knowledge economy is one that frees itself from the defects of the economics inaugurated by marginalism without repeating the mistakes of pre-marginalist theory. The single greatest source of insights and methods for the achievement of this goal is established economics itself. The work done under its aegis is limited in the ways that I have discussed. For all its failings, however, it remains our most powerful set of ideas about the economy. To accomplish the task, we need to redress its deficiencies without dispensing with its help.

We can undertake this effort in more than one way. We can do it as comprehensive or as fragmentary theory. And we can work from within or from outside established economics and its community of discourse. We can combine these intellectual options in different ways.

The intellectual alternative can take the form of a comprehensive theoretical project. In its most ambitious form, such a project would continue where Smith and Marx left off, retaking the concerns of classical economics without its overstatement of the importance of coercion and its understatement of the role of the imagination in economic life and without its necessitarian illusions about regimes, structural discontinuity, and structural alternatives. It would aspire to be what the economics of Smith and Marx was: social theory applied to the phenomena of production and exchange. Such an intellectual alternative, developed as comprehensive theory, can also result from a movement within economics, like the movement that produced marginalism at the end of the nineteenth century or like Keynes's limited heresy in the middle of the twentieth century.

Comprehensive theory will always be exceptional, whether or not it takes the established economics as its point of departure. The normal way to change the course of economic theory, from within economics or from outside it, is fragmentary rather than comprehensive. It develops new ideas and methods as they are needed to explore a particular problem, such as the confinement of the most advanced practice of production to insular vanguards and to technological and entrepreneurial elites.

It can achieve depth despite its fragmentary character to the extent that it focuses on the relation of the phenomena of production and exchange to their institutional back-ground—the economic regime—rather than taking the present arrangements of the market as natural and necessary. The imagination of radical reform—the piecemeal but potentially cumulative change of the established structure—is its foremost theoretical and practical interest. Its intellectual as well as its practical political hopes lie in the marriage of fragmentary theory to radical reform.

This book is an example of fragmentary theory. It explores and exemplifies a way of thinking. On the basis of that way of thinking, it proposes radical reforms in the organization of the economy, to be achieved piecemeal. It looks to the marriage of fragmentary theory and radical reform. It offers no general account of the economy and its transformation. However, by addressing its theme—the character and alternative futures of knowledge-intensive production—it finds itself called to suggest some of the elements of an alternative direction in our ideas about the economy.

Whether the theorizing is comprehensive or fragmentary, we can begin to carry out the task from within the specialized discourse and the professional world of economics or from outside them: from inside out, or from outside in.

To perform the task from inside economics need not mean to surrender to the now dominant ideas and methods. It should mean to use them and resist and revise them at the same time. To deny that such a practice of qualified engagement is possible in economics would be to suppose that the marginalists set the direction of economics for all time. It would be to fear that we cannot repeat their example of intellectual rebellion and redirection. It is also to slight the diversity of the history of economics, exemplified by the late nineteenth-century rivals to the marginalist program such as Edgeworth's treatment of economics as a psychological science in the tradition of Bentham or Marshall's proposal to develop economics as a science of loosely connected and context-bound causal sequences in the manner of natural history and by analogy to the science of tides or of the weather.

Under this practice of fragmentary theory from the inside, the thinker must engage the specialized discipline on its own terms (for it will refuse to rise to his) and by its own standards, including those of its mathematics and of its model-building, while holding himself to different terms and higher standards. He must show the steps by which the established economics can expand its vision, enlarge its tools, and relate insight into the actual and imagination of the adjacent possible, given that to understand something is always to grasp what it can become. Even if his intentions are revolutionary, he must in effect practice radical reform in the domain of ideas and then use these ideas as a guide to radical reform in the realm of practice. He may even find it useful to present his ideas in two versions: one in the mode acceptable to the established field and another freer from its restraints.

Such a standard can be met only with difficulty, hardship, and sacrifice. It is bound to cause trouble to those who try to satisfy it. If, however, the effort succeeds, if not immediately, then at least by the opinion of a later time, its effect can be lasting and far-reaching. The reward for engagement with the demanding discipline, and its practices and methods, is the development of a way of thinking in which many can share, rather than its consignment to the speculations of philosophers.

The way from the inside out and beyond is never the only way to address a major problem in economics such as the nature and alternative futures of the knowledge economy. Economics should be the study of the economy, not the study of the method pioneered by the marginalists. It will always be possible to do economics in ways that its professional practitioners would not recognize as economics and prefer to describe, if they engage it at all, as philosophy or social theory.

The appeal of this work from the outside is that it has no need to say only what can be said in the discourse of the established economics. But this advantage is likely to count for little if the work from outside economics fails to generate rigorous standards of its own and to find expression in an intellectual practice in which many can share without requiring genius as the condition of their engagement. It will also be unlikely to achieve anything of value if ambition, vanity, and ignorance mislead it into understating the achievements of the established economics and the value of its insights and methods to those who would rebel, from the outside, against it.

Consider, as an example, the vexed question of the role of mathematics in economic theory. In the analytic practice inaugurated by the marginalists, mathematics acquired a central function: it served as the favored instrument of a practice of economics, one that was closer to logic than to causal science. In the model-building into which post-marginalist economics devolved, mathematics remained the fundamental tool, exposing the implications of each model of a piece of economic activity on the basis of factual stipulations and causal theories, as well as in the light of normative commitments, supplied from outside the apparatus of economic analysis.

In the economics to which this book and the preceding discussion of economics and its history point, the place of mathematics is open. The use of mathematics would need to have a much more intimate relation to causal inquiry than it does in established economics, anticipating and provoking causal views, as mathematics has in the history of fundamental physics, not just representing them retrospectively. Mathematics would sometimes be useful and sometimes not. The limit of its usefulness would lie in the exploration of what is qualitative rather than quantitative (as in the discontinuities among different levels of breakthrough of the demand-side and the supply-side constraints on growth); in what depends on historical path dependence rather than on timeless economic truth; and in what involves institutional structure and institutional change rather than the allocation and reallocation of resources with a given institutional framework.

Such an economics would use mathematics more selectively than the established practice of economic analysis does. It would have little use for the relatively primitive mathematics (almost all of it developed before the middle of the nineteenth century) favored by the mathematics-venerating economics of today. It would require the higher mathematics that could bring the mathematical representation of economic activity closer to the frontier of the qualitative, the structural, and the historical.

This book is an example of fragmentary rather than of comprehensive theory and of the way from outside rather than from inside the established economics. It would be sheer dogmatism to affirm the precedence of one of these ways over the other: the comprehensive over the fragmentary, the outside path over the inside one, or vice versa. Each of these approaches has advantages and disadvantages. We should want each of them to count on its theoreticians and practitioners. Then we can judge each approach by the insights that it makes possible. We can avoid ranking these ways of changing economics by a scorecard that brings the study of the economy down to the level of our sense of what each of us does best.

19.

The Higher Purpose of the Inclusive Knowledge Economy

The insularity of the most advanced practice of production contributes to an evil distinct from the evils of economic stagnation and inequality. By condemning the vast majority of the labor force in even the richest countries, with the most educated populations, to less productive jobs, it also belittles them. It forces them to live diminished lives, giving inadequate scope to the development of their powers and to the expression of their humanity. To overcome the evil of belittlement through the transformation of workday experience is the higher purpose of an inclusive knowledge economy.

It is true that many who remain outside the knowledge economy in its present quarantined form may escape belittlement in jobs that require them to care for other people. This caring economy, however, can also be transformed, and better empower both its beneficiaries and its agents, if it takes on features of the now most advanced practice of production.

One way to deepen insight into the larger value of a deepened and widespread form of the knowledge economy is to consider and criticize the views of Marx and Keynes about the place of economic activity in the self-construction of humanity. Both Marx and Keynes foresaw a conquest of scarcity in the near future and viewed it as a decisive turn in the history of mankind. Both of them believed that the overcoming of scarcity would allow us to cast off the hateful burden of the need to work for a livelihood—the sustenance of the individual and of society. Both of them thought that productive labor was an instrumental imperative: inescapable only until the reign of scarcity had come to an end.

For the Keynes of *Economic Possibilities for Our Grandchildren* the coming supersession of scarcity will allow us to devote ourselves to private sublimities—the highest form of experience—rather than to waste ourselves on work performed under pressure of economic necessity. For the Marx of *The German Ideology* and of *Introduction to the Critique of the Gotha Program* the development of the forces of production, made possible by the ordeal of the sequence of modes of production, will conclude with the abolition of scarcity. The abolition of scarcity will spell the end of class society: the class structure has been necessary to ensure the coercive extraction of a surplus over current consumption. Once its functional basis in the constraint of scarcity disappears, there need no longer be a division of labor that forces each individual to mutilate himself by devoting most of his time to express, by force of economic necessity, only one aspect of his humanity. We will make ourselves whole again.

In the remaining pages of this book I give reasons to reject both this view of scarcity and this conception of work. We have no grounds to expect that mankind will overcome scarcity in any foreseeable future. However, the need to continue working in the shadow of scarcity need not result in a diminishment of our prospects. Under a deepened and disseminated form of the knowledge economy, we can expect more from labor than the instrumental view of work allows. By reconsidering those themes in Marx's and Keynes's ideas we can gain greater clarity about the higher purpose of inclusive vanguardism.

There are three reasons to doubt that the burden of scarcity will be lifted anytime soon. The knowledge economy holds the potential of relaxing or even reversing the constraint of diminishing marginal returns to increases in any input in the process of production. The achievement of this potential, however, does not spell the end of scarcity. Even the spread of knowledge-intensive production throughout much of the economy will not be enough.

One reason to expect the persistence of scarcity is that all historical societies continuously generate new forms of subjugation and exclusion even as they redress older forms. They do so as a consequence of the struggle for power within and among states. Scarcity will exist for the losers even when it no longer haunts the winners. An example is the rise of precarious employment in the wake of the decline of mass production.

Our best prospect today of preventing the recurrence of subjugation and exclusion in new forms, while accelerating economic growth, is to combine the advancement of inclusive vanguardism in the economy with the development of a high-energy democracy in politics. But this is a direction rather than a safe house. We can expect to be surprised along the way by new turns in the struggle for power, whether between capital and labor or in other forms, and new instances of entrenched advantage and disadvantage.

The perpetual creation of inequality is aggravated by the Malthusian element in economic history. The victims of this ordeal may have children not only as safeguards against economic insecurity in old age but also as tokens of hope. Fecundity will then delay—even indefinitely—the day when scarcity will have been overcome.

A second reason to anticipate a long afterlife for scarcity is the mimetic and insatiable character of desire and consumption, for the affirmation of which the knowledge economy creates greater opportunity. One of the traits of the knowledge economy, even at the relatively superficial level of production engineering, is to allow for the destandardization or customization of goods and services and for a mass market in such products, at widely accessible prices rather than in the small-scale and relatively expensive form of craft manufacture.

This characteristic potential of advanced manufacturing and knowledge-deep services gives more room to mimetic desire. To a large extent, we want what others want. Beyond the bare necessities of the preservation and reproduction of life, human desire has no fixed content. It is easily kidnaped by the example of others, which gives it the content that it lacks. The customization that is enabled by the new most advanced practice of production makes it possible for there to be more that can be desired, and more desire to imitate, while maintaining under the disguise of imitation the semblance of individual craving.

Human desire is not just mimetic; it is also empty, roving, and insatiable. It is insatiable because in fixing, beyond the requirements of sustenance, on particular objects, it wants them as down payments on what no good or service can assure us of: that each of us is who he takes himself to be and that there is an unconditional place for him in the world. We seek the unlimited from the limited, the absolute from the conditional, and the eternal from the transient. We cannot get what we want. The frustration of our desire to get from particulars what they cannot give us condemns us forever to restart the chase. And the novel features of production in the age of the knowledge economy multiply excuses to continue the pursuit.

If desire is insatiable, scarcity can have no end: there will never be enough of what we want. Scarcity can be measured only relative to desire. Unlimited desire will not mean unlimited demand: for demand is the translation of desire into purchasing power. There is thus no contradiction in treating desire as unlimited while recognizing that there are demand as well as supply constraints on economic growth and that a breakthrough of supply-side limits on economic growth does not ensure a corresponding breakthrough on demand-side limits.

A third reason for the indefinite survival of scarcity is the greater relative importance, in the societies in which the knowledge economy emerges, of a subset of desires and demands: those that have to do with our claims on one another's personalized service and attention. Our appetite for things, even when customized, may eventually decline. Machines may take away many of the jobs of those who produce them. There is no limit, however, to our desire for service and attention from one another. If they are not freely given to us, we will set out to buy them. Every particular benefit that we secure from the other person will stand as a proxy for what each of us most wants: assurance that there he has a home in the world, a basis for self-acceptance and acceptance by others.

The increasing relative importance of the services that we can render to one another guarantees that scarcity will not end. We can never get enough of the finite stock of services that is available, because every service performs both its immediate and visible function and an ulterior role, as a token of the unconditional place in the world that we seek. Our need for attention would be no less insatiable in an economy in which economically dependent wage labor had given way to a combination of self-employment and cooperation as the predominant form of free work.

Robinson Crusoe on his island accumulated things to diminish his dependence on people and to make up for their absence in his life. He did what we all do: he made the accumulation of things serve as a functional substitute for dependence on people. The flawed and unsatisfactory character of the substitution soon becomes clear. Even Robinson Crusoe needed Friday and plotted to return home. Even he wanted to replace the accumulation of things with the society of his friends and countrymen.

The rise and spread of the knowledge economy fails to alter these facts. It lends them even more force. It does so in one way by causing a shift of labor from advanced manufacturing to personalized services. It does so in another way by the cumulative effect of greater collective and individual wealth on our need for more things, which it attenuates over time, and on our need for people and their services, which it increases.

Contrary to what Marx and Keynes supposed, we have no prospect of overcoming scarcity, although the significance of scarcity may change under a form of production that loosens or reverses the constraint of diminishing marginal returns, which has up to now remained the most persistent and universal regularity of economic life. Neither, however, should we accept the instrumental view of work, under any established division of labor. The instrumental conception of labor was the one that Marx and Keynes took for granted, seeing work in the production system as brute necessity, imposed on us by scarcity and diverting us from our greater possibilities.

This idea of work amounts to a species of world abandonment. It despairs of seeing the higher attributes of our humanity expressed in our material life unless and until the weight of scarcity has been lifted. The ideal of work that enables us to build and to change ourselves by trying to change a piece of the world seems, according to this idea, pertinent only to a society in which material needs have ceased to bind us to the wheel of production. Until then, even the advantaged will be unfree; they will be consumed by the struggle to maintain their privilege and exercise the powers accompanying it, unless they are isolated artists or thinkers living as apostates from the social order. These happy few will require insight, virtue, and luck to remain uncorrupted by their advantages.

Economic life, understood in this way, is always a terrain of constraint. Freedom is freedom from the economy rather than freedom in the economy.

No economic regime or practice of production offers freedom without constraint. However, the extent to which production can become a field of freedom as well as of constraint varies from one economic and political regime to another, and from one practice of production to another. As it deepens and spreads, by the means and in the direction that I have described, the knowledge economy ascends the ladder of openness to experiences of freedom. It does so more through its deeper characteristics—its potential for increasing returns, its reshaping of production as discovery, and its heightening of trust and discretion—than on account of its superficial traits—those that it displays in its present insular form. It does more by virtue of the cognitive-educational, social-moral, and legal-institutional requirements of its deepening and dissemination than as a consequence of those deeper characteristics. And it does so more as an effect of the background conditions favorable to fulfilling those requirements—the radicalization of the experimentalist impulse in culture and high-energy democracy in politics—than as a result of their fulfillment.

It is less the knowledge economy, viewed apart as a practice of production, that has the potential to offer freedom within rather than from the economy than it is the larger movement in practice and in thought from which the advancement of the knowledge economy must come. The further away we move from the work of production to its supportive setting, the greater becomes the potential to shift the balance between constraint and freedom in economic life. It is the total package—the practice of production in the context of the inducements to the achievement of its distant potential—that holds the emancipatory promise.

Consider the content of this promise from two complementary standpoints: the nature and status of labor and the relation of the practice of production to our mental experience.

There have been three main conceptions of work in the history of civilization. The first two have shadowed mankind throughout history. The third is a recent, revolutionary invention. The first is the instrumental view of work: work as what the vast majority of people have had to undertake in the unequal societies, bent under the yoke of scarcity, that history has seen. Relief and humanity will lie elsewhere: in family life and in personal relations outside the prison house of unavoidable labor.

The second is the idea of work as an honorable calling: a station, a profession, a specialty in the social division of labor, affording respect and self-respect as well as a livelihood. To occupy such a station is to reconcile material and moral need, albeit at the cost of accepting a set of stable routines and a predefined role in society and the economy. It is to accept the inevitability of a mutilation: that to be something in society we turn ourselves into someone in particular, accepting a rigidly confined place in the division of labor and foregoing the selves that we might have become.

The third is the idea of the transformative vocation: an invention of the age of democracy and of romanticism, carried later to the whole world on the wings of global romantic culture and the political doctrines of liberalism, socialism, and democracy. By seeking to change part of the world around us, we make ourselves greater and freer. We affirm our transcendence over station and circumstance.

We refuse the last word to the social and conceptual worlds that we inhabit and keep the last word for ourselves.

To live the idea of the transformative vocation, not just to entertain it as a fantasy, has remained the prerogative of a tiny elite of innovators and leaders. Yet the knowledge economy holds the promise of making this experience available to many. It cannot do so in its present insular form. Moreover, its prospect of keeping that promise depends on the movement toward deepening and spreading the most advanced practice of production. Among the requirements for this movement, the one bearing most directly on this hope is change in the legal status of labor: the gradual replacement of economically dependent wage work by the combination of self-employment (not as disguised wage work) and cooperation (organized by alternative property regimes). These and other changes in the arrangements of the economy, the character of education, and the organization of politics determine whether the idea of the transformative vocation can live in economic reality.

To the extent that it does live, it holds the prospect of sharing in a basic aspect of freedom: our ability to empower ourselves by turning the tables on the habitual framework of our activity. Freedom, in its most radical and comprehensive meaning, is affirming, in deeds not words, that there is more in us—in each of us individually and in all of us collectively—than there is or even can be in the social and conceptual worlds that we build and join and in the roles that we perform.

As it deepens and spreads, the knowledge economy makes the practice of production more closely resemble the workings of the imagination. Remember the conception of the duality of the mind. In one of its aspects, the mind resembles a machine: it is formulaic. But in another aspect, the mode of the imagination, the mind is an anti-machine: it pushes ahead by defying its own settled presuppositions and by outreaching the methods on which it habitually relies. It discovers more than it can yet shape and justify. It distances itself from the immediate phenomenon and grasps it by subsuming it under a range of variations—of what the object of its attention could become in the realm of the adjacent possible.

Imagination is freedom because it is transcendence in the workings of the mind. A form of production giving more space to the imagination than any previous practice of production ever gave represents an advance in freedom. It justifies the hope that we might find freedom in the economy rather than only freedom from the economy.

A knowledge economy in which many can take part does more than increase productivity and diminish inequality. It has the potential to lift us up together, to offer us a shared bigness. Viewed from the perspective of its advent, the record of our material life is the history of the long, halting triumph of the imagination.

Index

administrative Fordism, 86–87, 110, 185, 187
agency, 8, 145
  enhancement of, 188, 214
agriculture
  market and, 210–11
  mass production and, 87–88
  scientific, 6, 53, 88, 163
  transferring resources to industry from, 12, 15, 85–86, 161, 219
  in US, 88, 209–10
Alphabet (company), 59
antitrust law, 66–67
artificial intelligence, 2, 21, 41, 42, 94, 223

belated Fordism, 15, 165, 166–67
Bentham, Jeremy, 229, 273
bilateral executory contract, 48, 102, 222, 245
Brazil, 164–70
  entrepreneurial impulse in, 166, 168–69
  industry in, 164–66
Britain, 32, 151, 210–11

capital
  access to, 119, 123, 125, 184
  human, 160
  labor's relations with, 63–64, 184–86, 221, 224–25
  providers and takers of, 221
  social, 49–51, 105
  venture, 119–20, 194
capital appreciation, 58
capitalism
  inclusive knowledge economy and, 236–37
  Marx on, 32, 172, 210, 237, 266, 268
  moral presuppositions of, 47–48
  no in-built structure of, 179–80, 228, 236

  "varieties of," 179, 228
  See also market economy and order
China, 55, 141, 162, 199
Christensen, Clayton, 216
civil society, 110, 134
  government and, 87, 157, 187
classical economics. *See* economics – classical
closed-list thesis, 118, 235
coercion, 266–68
cognitive psychology, 42
collective bargaining, 64, 102
collective dictatorship, 140–41
collective difference, 148–49
combined and uneven development, 90, 137, 172, 186
comparative advantage doctrine, 253
compensatory and corrective redistribution
  demand constraints and, 205–8
  market economy and, 73–74
  progressive taxation, 73, 74, 76, 78–80, 182, 205, 208
  public spending, 205, 207–8
  social entitlements and transfers, 64, 73–75, 76, 248
  tax-and-transfer, 13, 64, 78, 207, 209
competition
  cooperation and, 49, 67, 103, 133–34
  between large and small firms, 59–60
  market, 253–56
competitive selection, 253–56
consumption
  growth of, 53
  individual desire and, 239, 280
  mass, 176, 204–5
  surplus over current, 9, 32, 266, 278
  taxes on, 75, 77–78, 79, 208
contract and property law, 48, 102, 109, 124

292